KJV DEVOTIONAL for Women

Suzanne Hadley Gosselin
and Carolyn Hadley

HARVEST HOUSE PUBLISHERS
EUGENE, OREGON

Cover design by Dugan Design Group
Cover photo © Svetlana Lukienko / Adobe Stock
Interior design by KUHN Design Group

For bulk, special sales, or ministry purchases, please call 1-800-547-8979.
Email: Customerservice@hhpbooks.com

M This logo is a federally registered trademark of the Hawkins Children's LLC. Harvest House Publishers, Inc., is the exclusive licensee of this trademark.

KJV Devotional for Women

Copyright © 2022 by Harvest House Publishers
Published by Harvest House Publishers
Eugene, Oregon 97408
www.harvesthousepublishers.com

ISBN 978-0-7369-8490-4 (hardcover)
ISBN 978-0-7369-8492-8 (eBook)

Printed in China

22 23 24 25 26 27 28 29 30 / RDS / 10 9 8 7 6 5 4 3 2

INTRODUCTION

The King James Bible is the longest-enduring and best-selling English version of the Bible. In 1604, King James I authorized its creation, and after seven years of translation work by fifty-four translators and scholars, it was completed in 1611. At the time it was created, the KJV was significant because of the collaborative process of its creation, which utilized and united opposing theological factions.

The King James Bible has enjoyed an illustrious career, influencing language, literature, and culture. Almost every American president has been sworn into office with his hand on a King James Bible, and more than 250 common English phases originate from the version. The KJV contains more than 788,000 words, with 12,000 of them being unique.

This devotional is written by two women: Suzanne Gosselin, a pastor's wife and stay-at-home mother of four children, and her aunt, Carolyn Hadley, a retired nurse, widow, mother of three, and grandmother of six.

Both women wanted to honor the tradition of the King James Bible, writing reflections based on verses they have known and loved since childhood. Each reflection has been labeled with the author's name for clarity. The authors pray that as you meditate on these well-loved passages of Scripture and the truths they contain, the God of hope will fill you with all joy and peace in believing (Romans 15:13).

REMINDERS OF THE CREATOR

Suzanne

*All things were made by him; and without
him was not any thing made that was made.*
JOHN 1:3

A few years ago, we were leaving church, and I noticed my young daughter grasping handfuls of leaves, sticks, and pebbles.

"What is that?" I asked her.

"I'm keeping all of these things because they remind me of God," she said.

I was struck by her simple observation. Nature is a powerful reminder that Jesus, through God, created and controls all things. Nothing we see would exist without Him.

This truth brings comfort when the world seems out of control. When I feel overwhelmed by the news headlines or a challenging situation in my own life, I can remember that everything that exists is here because of my loving, powerful Creator. When I wonder if the Lord will come through for me, I need only look at an intricate leaf, a blooming flower, or a towering grove of trees to see what He has already done and trust that my circumstances are in His capable hands.

SOUL SUPPORT

Suzanne

And the LORD commanded us to do all these statutes,
to fear the LORD our God, for our good always,
that he might preserve us alive, as it is at this day.
DEUTERONOMY 6:24

Not long ago I was in a buffet line at a women's event. I noticed the woman next to me taking only a few raspberries when there were luscious egg dishes and pastries spread across the table.

"Are you on a restrictive diet?" I asked, feeling a bit sorry for her. Her reply took me aback.

"I prefer not to think of it as a restrictive diet," she said cheerfully. "I just eat what is supportive to my body."

How many times do you and I think of God's commands as restrictive? We may feel like abiding by His statutes sucks the fun out of life or is a sacrifice. But that's the wrong way to look at it.

God's commands are life-giving and supportive to our souls. In some cases, they preserve our physical lives, but they always enrich our spiritual lives. As I follow Jesus, I'm not giving up something; I'm choosing to pursue that which causes my soul to flourish.

THE WELLNESS DIET

Carolyn

Whether therefore ye eat, or drink, or
whatsoever ye do, do all to the glory of God.
1 CORINTHIANS 10:31

I have an unusual New Year's tradition. I literally "jump" into the next year by leaping off a stool, chair, or hearth. This was my mother-in-law's way of signaling a fresh, new start to the year. Every January, I honor her memory by doing this activity, and I hope to pass this tradition down to future generations.

A new year offers hope for positive change. My goals are to be physically and spiritually fit so I can serve the Lord to the best of my ability. This requires self-discipline and a healthy lifestyle of adequate sleep, reduced stress, and exercise.

More importantly, a new year offers me an opportunity to become more spiritually fit by surrendering myself more to Christ. I do this as I seek Him daily and allow Him to feed my soul. It may not be a new year, but why not glorify God by jumping into habits that support your physical and spiritual health?

GOD'S GOOD VOICE

Suzanne

My sheep hear my voice, and I know them, and they follow me.
JOHN 10:27

When my son was four years old, he paid me an unusual compliment. "You're my best mom," he said. "Your voice sounds good."

As I pondered his simple words, I reflected that I also love *my* mother's voice. I have often called her just to hear her reassuring voice on the other end of the line. The Bible says God's sheep, believers, hear His voice and follow Him. His voice should sound attractive because He is a good and loving Father, a gentle Shepherd, and a faithful yokefellow.

The longer I walk with the Lord, the more familiar His still, small voice becomes. I hear it when my soul is overwhelmed and fearful. I hear it when I step out into His creation and see His glory. I hear it in the intimate moments where I confess something no human knows about me and hear Him say, "I love you." May I learn to listen well, and may my Shepherd's voice be a delight to hear.

LIVING HOW WE OUGHT

Suzanne

*For the grace of God that bringeth salvation hath
appeared to all men, teaching us that, denying
ungodliness and worldly lusts, we should live soberly,
righteously, and godly, in this present world; looking
for that blessed hope, and the glorious appearing
of the great God and our Savior Jesus Christ.*
TITUS 2:11-13

When we look at the world around us, there are many messages telling us how we ought to live. *Do what makes you happy,* some cry. *Do what makes other people happy,* others shout. The competing voices in our culture can make us feel tossed in the waves of popular opinion and worldly wisdom. Sometimes it's hard to know where to turn our eyes, where we should focus.

Paul answered this very question when he told Titus how the saved should live in light of God's grace. The unmerited gift of salvation should motivate us to turn away from ungodliness and live measured, righteous lives in Christ. And as we do, we look forward to a great hope—the day the trials of this life are over and our risen Savior returns to make all things new.

The Lone Seagull

Carolyn

*Be sober, be vigilant; because your adversary
the devil, as a roaring lion, walketh
about, seeking whom he may devour.*
1 PETER 5:8

A few years ago, my family took a beach vacation to Florida. One morning, I took in the beautiful panorama from the balcony of our condo. The reflection of the blue-green water, the waves crashing on the white sandy shoreline, the swaying palm trees, and the jabbering of seagulls all fought for my attention and delighted my senses.

Just then, I noticed a lone seagull hovering in the air at a distance behind a colony of seagulls flying in *V* formation. *Had it been late in joining the group?* I wondered. *Was it rejected by others? Or did it want to be the leader and refuse to fall in line?* Whatever the reason, this seagull was on a solo flight.

As believers, we may sometimes feel as if we're flying solo. But there is strength in numbers. Flying alone can be a liability. We can find protection and strength in God and His people. We must keep watch for Satan's attempts to undermine God's purposes in our lives. And the safest place to do that is in Christian community. God grants us strength in numbers.

Two Are Better Than One

Suzanne

Two are better than one; because they have a good reward for their labor. For if they fall, the one will lift up his fellow: but woe to him that is alone when he falleth; for he hath not another to help him up.

ECCLESIASTES 4:9-10

One of the most uncomfortable things for me is needing help. I greatly prefer to handle problems on my own rather than have my weaknesses revealed. But sometimes a second person is not only helpful but absolutely necessary!

God designed us to be interdependent. This is seen in how He established families at the start of creation and how He designed the church to function—a diverse body of believers working together to accomplish God's purposes. We need other people to help and encourage us. Think of a situation where you simply could not have gotten by without another's help. How did God use that person in your life? How can you support someone today?

BE KIND

Suzanne

*And be ye kind one to another, tenderhearted,
forgiving one another, even as God for
Christ's sake hath forgiven you.*
EPHESIANS 4:32

Not long ago, I stepped into line at a convenience store just as a young man with cerebral palsy approached the counter in a motorized wheelchair. Over the next few minutes, I watched the cashier patiently help the man purchase a soft drink, leaning in to understand his slurred speech.

Even though the man had difficulty with the steps of making his purchase, the other customers remained unbothered and even helped him retrieve his wallet to pay. When the purchase was complete, the cashier went above and beyond, pouring the man's soft drink into his insulated cup.

"Have a good day, everyone!" the man said as he wheeled away.

The situation touched me. It reminded me of God's kindness in saving me when I could do nothing for myself. When we show kindness to others, we not only make ourselves a blessing to our fellow man, but we also reflect the character of our compassionate God. That's a great reason to be kind today!

DECLARING MY PRAISE

Carolyn

Let everything that hath breath praise
the LORD. Praise ye the LORD.
PSALM 150:6

One summer evening, after enjoying a wonderful meal and sweet fellowship with a group of friends, my husband and I blended our voices with eight others to sing the doxology on the restaurant's front porch.

Praise God, from whom all blessings flow.
Praise Him, all creatures here below.
Praise Him above, ye heavenly host.
Praise Father, Son, and Holy Ghost.

These familiar words written by Thomas Ken make up one of the most widely sung hymns of all time. The song reminds us that all blessings and good gifts flow from God above. The doxology has become one of my family's favorite anthems to sing at family gatherings and holidays.

That evening on the restaurant porch, those who passed by asked if we were a choir, and we kindly told them no. We simply could not contain our praise! Two of those men, including my husband, have gone to be with the Lord since that night, but this sweet memory remains. As long as we have breath, may God find us faithful to give Him the praise He deserves.

FAITHFUL GOD

Suzanne

*If we believe not, yet he abideth
faithful: he cannot deny himself.*
2 TIMOTHY 2:13

Understanding God's faithfulness can be difficult at times because it is so contrary to our human expression of it. His commitment to His promises is integral to His character. It's impossible for Him to be anything but faithful.

The hymnist Thomas Chisholm put it beautifully in his famous hymn: "Great is Thy faithfulness, O God my Father / There is no shadow of turning with Thee / Thou changest not, Thy compassions, they fail not / As Thou hast been Thou forever wilt be."

Perhaps the greatest truth is that God's faithfulness is not dependent on my actions. I can think of many times I have been unfaithful. I have reneged on a promise, failed to trust God, or neglected to obey His commands. But when I fail to believe, God's character remains unchanged. As I realize this important truth, I am freed to rest on His character and trust in His work in my life.

Asking for Wisdom

— *Suzanne* —

If any of you lack wisdom, let him ask of
God, that giveth to all men liberally, and
upbraideth not; and it shall be given him.
JAMES 1:5

Have you ever been at a loss for what to do? Maybe you found yourself in the midst of a struggling relationship or needed insight on whether or not to take a new job. Perhaps you were confronted with two great options and had to choose between them.

God invites us to ask for wisdom. He doesn't condemn us for what we don't know or hold back His wisdom when we need it so desperately. Just the opposite! When we ask for wisdom, He gives it liberally without finding fault!

While seeking advice from a wise friend or family member may be our first inclination, God tells us we can come to Him directly—the very source of wisdom. Whatever situation you may be facing today, no matter how unlikely a solution may feel, God promises to give you wisdom when you ask. What are you waiting for?

FOLDED NAPKIN

— *Carolyn* —

*And the napkin, that was about his
head, not lying with the linen clothes, but
wrapped together in a place by itself.*
JOHN 20:7

When Peter and John arrived at the empty tomb that first Easter morning, an amazing site met their gaze. Inside the tomb, the disciples saw the linen graveclothes thrown to the side, while the cloth that had covered Jesus's face was folded neatly at the head of the stony grave.

In Jewish culture, a servant would prepare his master's dining table and watch, usually just out of sight, while his master ate his meal. When the master was done eating, he would leave a wadded napkin on the table that meant "I'm done." Then the servant could come and clear the table. However, if the master folded his napkin and left it on the table, that meant, "I'm not finished yet. I'm coming back!"

It seems that Jesus left a message of hope for His disciples and all believers that resurrection morning. Jesus came to be our risen Savior, but He will return as Judge and King. Jesus is coming back!

GREATEST TREASURE

Suzanne

Likewise, I say unto you, there is joy in the presence of the angels of God over one sinner that repenteth.
LUKE 15:10

I remember a Christmas shopping trip with my Aunt Carolyn and cousin Melissa, when I was a girl. At the end of a fun shopping day, Melissa realized she had left a twenty-dollar bill in the mall bathroom. Our hearts sank. Nearly an hour had gone by. Surely the cash would not still be there. But when we returned to the restroom, the twenty dollars was there, sitting on top of the toilet tissue dispenser. What joy and relief we all felt!

Jesus told a parable about a woman who had ten pieces of silver and lost one. The woman lit a candle, swept the house, and searched diligently until she found that one lost piece. Then she gathered her friends and neighbors to rejoice. When a sinner repents, Jesus explained, there is similar rejoicing in heaven.

When God draws a sinner to Himself, that event is truly deserving of rejoicing and celebration!

PATIENCE IN THE PROCESS

Suzanne

And let us not be weary in well doing: for in due season we shall reap, if we faint not.
GALATIANS 6:9

Planting and harvest were very familiar topics to first-century Middle Eastern people. Perhaps that's why the apostle Paul often used the analogy of farming to describe matters of faith. Like living for Jesus, farming is a process: There is a season to plant, a season to allow the seeds to grow, and a season to reap the harvest.

We live in a world that loves instant, or nearly instant, results, but living a life of obedience to Christ often requires perseverance to see the harvest. In fact, sometimes we may not even see what our good works have accomplished this side of heaven. But God's Word encourages us to continue to do good without becoming weary.

Think of a situation in your life that requires perseverance. Ask God to give you strength to carry on as you trust in His promise of the harvest ahead.

CHOOSING THANKS

—————— *Carolyn* ——————

In every thing give thanks: for this is the will
of God in Christ Jesus concerning you.
1 THESSALONIANS 5:18

Giving thanks after the death of my husband and mother was emotionally challenging. Because they were believers, I have the confident hope of a future heavenly reunion. And since the loss, God, my protector and provider, has been ministering to my emotional, physical, and spiritual needs daily. My weaknesses have become strengths, as I have trusted His guidance and felt His loving care.

As I continue on this life journey, I must remember I am not alone. God has promised to never leave or forsake me. He is my constant and faithful companion. My faith is growing, and I find comfort and peace in Him and His precious Word.

I have found that as I choose thanks in everything, I don't have room for complaining or ongoing disappointment. God's plan becomes my plan, and I anticipate with great joy the abundant life God has in store for me. For me, choosing thanksgiving has been my defining moment.

SHORTCOMINGS ERASED

Suzanne

*As far as the east is from the west, so far hath
he removed our transgressions from us.*
PSALM 103:12

One night I walked into my eight-year-old daughter's room where she was sitting on her bed, head down. A few minutes earlier, I had too quickly judged a skirmish among my children and chastised her for something she didn't do. I felt terrible.

I sat down beside her on the bed and said I was sorry. I explained I had sinned in becoming so angry and apologized for my harsh words. She forgave me, but inside I felt condemned. This wasn't the first time I'd lost my temper, and I knew it wouldn't be the last.

The psalmist offers hope when he describes how completely God forgives my sin. Whether a passing moment of selfishness or a violation of one of the "Thou Shalt Nots," no transgression is too great to be completely forgiven by God through the blood of Christ Jesus. As a human, I will miss the mark, but God, in His mercy, removes all evidence of my sin. Praise Him!

SEEKING WITH MY WHOLE HEART

Suzanne

And ye shall seek me, and find me, when ye
shall search for me with all your heart.
JEREMIAH 29:13

The Bible is filled with the promises of God. But this little gem found in the book of Jeremiah is one of the sweetest I've found: "Ye shall seek me, and find me." God can be found! He is not a cosmic watchmaker who stands at a distance with little care for what happens in the lives of humans. He wants to be personally involved in our lives.

The promise that we will find God is contingent on the second half of the verse: "when ye shall search for me with all your heart." God knows our propensity for divided hearts. We so easily search for fulfillment in worldly things. But God asks that we come to Him first with our whole hearts, proclaiming that we want what only He can give. In so doing, we will find Him close at hand, ready to provide everything we need. That's a promise I need to remember daily.

DIVINE APPOINTMENTS

Carolyn

*And he said unto them, Go ye into all the
world, and preach the gospel to every creature.*
MARK 16:15

A widow I know shares her faith daily, using gospel
bracelets and tracts. She calls those she meets and
talks to "divine appointments." These regular "appointments" are people whom God has prepared to hear the
truth about Jesus's saving grace from my faithful friend.
The recipients of the good news are all different—a cashier,
a stranger in a restaurant, or someone walking near my
friend's home.

Those of us who have accepted Christ's personal gift of
salvation have already experienced that "divine appointment"—maybe with an equipped saint who followed
Christ's mandate to preach the gospel.

We are now qualified to share the simple plan of salvation with others. We can tell them of God's invitation
to admit their sin, repent, and believe in Jesus, the Son
of God, who was born of a virgin, died sacrificially, was
buried, and rose again. Just as we have, they can call on
the name of the Lord and accept God's free gift of salvation and eternal life through faith in God. Our world desperately needs this hope. Ask the Lord to show you the
"divine appointments" He has for you today.

FINDING PEACE

Suzanne

---

*Be careful for nothing; but in every thing by prayer
and supplication with thanksgiving let your
requests be made known unto God. And the peace
of God, which passeth all understanding, shall
keep your hearts and minds through Christ Jesus.*
PHILIPPIANS 4:6-7

I lie awake well after midnight, the cares of the day playing through my anxious mind. How could I possibly solve all the problems before me? Financial stresses, decisions for my children's schooling, and health concerns threatened to overwhelm me.

I've heard it said, "Worry is like a rocking chair; it gives you something to do but never gets you anywhere." When I get stuck in the rocking chair of worry, I become focused on my fears instead of God's provision.

These verses provide the antidote to worry: prayer and thanksgiving. When I pour out my cares to God, He steps in with unlimited resources to help me. And as I thank Him for what He's already done, He opens my eyes to His tender care. The next time you're rocking in that worry, begin with prayer and thankfulness. Then trust God to provide His perfect peace.

GOD'S LOVING CORRECTION

Suzanne

For whom the Lord loveth he chasteneth, and
scourgeth every son whom he receiveth.
HEBREWS 12:6

One day my third-grade daughter came to me and told me an obvious lie. I had knowledge that completely contradicted her untruth. When I caught her in her lie, she became flustered and then looked at the floor in embarrassment and frustration.

"Sadie," I said. "God loves you. That's why He allowed you to get caught. He knows lies are a trap, and He wants you to always tell the truth."

My daughter nodded her head and came over for a hug.

I was well down the road of faith when I realized that "getting caught" in sin is a mercy from the Lord. Sin being exposed often begins the process of repentance and healing. The Lord's chastening in my life is evidence of His love for me and His desire that I experience the blessings that come from living a righteous life. This correction may be painful in the moment, but I can still run into my loving Father's arms, knowing I will be welcomed.

BLIND FAITH

Carolyn

For we walk by faith, not by sight.
2 CORINTHIANS 5:7

I have a sweet sister in the Lord who has been blind since birth. Throughout her life journey, she has been demonstrating her faith—in God and others. She waits with great anticipation for her sight to be restored, knowing the first face she will see will be the face of Jesus.

I have had the privilege of "being her eyes," guiding her through stores, restaurants, and church while she simply holds onto my arm and listens to my voice. Every time she buckles her seat belt in my car, she has faith I will drive her safely to her destination. Even though she lacks sight, my friend has never given up; her faith in God is strengthened daily.

As a believer, I desire an enduring faith, where I am fully trusting and relying on God, His Word, and His promises. My friend is a beautiful picture of trusting God when I cannot see how He is working or understand His movements. Like my friend, I look forward to the day I will see my Savior face-to-face and *see* how He was tenderly leading me all along.

STRIVING FOR UNITY

Suzanne

*Finally, brethren, farewell. Be perfect, be of
good comfort, be of one mind, live in peace; and
the God of love and peace shall be with you.*
2 CORINTHIANS 13:11

As a pastor's wife, I often have a front-row seat to divisions among believers. Because churches are full of imperfect sinners, conflicts are guaranteed to arise. And sometimes these skirmishes can become quite ugly. But consider Paul's farewell benediction to the church in Corinth. He prioritizes peace, comfort, and unity.

These things aren't just part of a pipe dream either. As we seek these things, God will come alongside us, providing His love and peace. When conflicts arise, I can ask God for wisdom to live in peace with fellow Christians. That doesn't mean I won't have to take a stand for something I believe or seek biblical reconciliation with someone in the family of God. But the purpose of these actions should always be to create greater peace and unity among the brethren.

At times, promoting unity may seem like a daunting task, but it's one God promises to bless.

PREPARED FOR BATTLE

Suzanne

*For the weapons of our warfare are not
carnal, but mighty through God to
the pulling down of strong holds.*

2 CORINTHIANS 10:4

My husband loves a good war movie. He's drawn to the stories of courage, bravery, and brotherhood. There's something so inspiring about rooting for the righteous to prevail.

Scripture tells us that as believers, we are in a battle. When the struggles common to man enter our lives, we must remember there is a spiritual battle happening. The ordinary defenses of our strength, smarts, and resources will not help us win this battle. Instead, God provides us with His mighty weapons that can tear down strongholds and even bring our thought life under His control.

Our adversary, the Devil, doesn't stand a chance against the powerful weapons God gives us. Furthermore, we already know who wins the battle! Remember today that you do not go into battle unarmed. God has provided you with everything you need to fight and win, including His own presence.

LOCATION, LOCATION, LOCATION!

Carolyn

In my Father's house are many mansions: if it
were not so, I would have told you. I go to prepare
a place for you. And if I go and prepare a place
for you, I will come again, and receive you unto
myself; that where I am, there ye may be also.
JOHN 14:2-3

In the real estate business, you hear the most important
asset of a property is location. People want to be settled
in good school districts, close to work, near desired restaurants and parks, and in places with little crime. These
desires supersede style, landscaping, and amenities.

We have a choice to make regarding our eternal location. A place is being prepared both for those who trust in
Jesus and for those who follow their own desires and ultimately God's enemy, Satan. These destinations—heaven
and hell—are realities Scripture clearly communicates.

My future home, which is being lovingly prepared for
me, is secure because I have trusted Jesus as my Savior. In
this life, we elevate location, but we should also consider
our eternal setting. When we do, we will want to tell others about how they, too, can experience the best location
ever—eternity in God's glorious presence.

FEAR NOT

Suzanne

---

*Fear thou not; for I am with thee: be not
dismayed; for I am thy God: I will strengthen
thee; yea, I will help thee; yea, I will uphold
thee with the right hand of my righteousness.*

ISAIAH 41:10

What are your biggest fears? Maybe you worry about the health and safety of your loved ones. Perhaps you fear what might happen in the future. Maybe circumstances you cannot control are filling you with a sense of dread. Fear is a powerful motivator in this world. But when we allow our hearts and minds to be ruled by it, we lose sight of the One who holds all things together and has the power to intervene in any situation.

God is bigger than our fears. No matter how uncertain life is, He has sovereign control over all things. We can have courage and hope because He Himself promises to strengthen, help, and uphold us.

Whatever fear grips you today, remember who your God is. He is powerful enough to handle every anxiety and calm your worried heart.

A Love Poem

My beloved spake, and said unto me, Rise
up, my love, my fair one, and come away.
Song of Solomon 2:10

During college, my English professor asked us to write a poem about love. If he liked it, you would be exempt from the final exam. I took on the challenge and wrote a poem about my feelings for my high school sweetheart (who later became my husband). Here is an excerpt from "His Love" (which earned me the exemption):

Two people find oneness in being together and sharing together.

They sing the same melody, for their love brings a harmonious tune to their ears.

When they walk, their limbs move simultaneously, never missing a step in the love march.

When they smile, the world is perfect.

How can love be so beautiful, unique, and special?

Its source is God, the Omnipotent One.

For it is He who first loved, and He who first shared His love with another.

In Scripture, Solomon and the maiden affirm their love in poetic language, just as my poem expressed my love for my sweetheart. Our God is a romantic. He is love and allows us to love and be loved by others. This is a beautiful picture of His profound feelings for us.

IT'S GOING TO BE OKAY

Suzanne

And he is before all things, and
by him all things consist.
COLOSSIANS 1:17

What do you believe God isn't holding together in your life?"

My friend's question caught me off guard. I had been telling her of some of the hurts and fears I'd acquired during a tumultuous year dealing with a global pandemic. Everything felt out of whack. She reminded me that in the midst of feeling this way, I can have hope because I know the One *by whom all things consist.*

That doesn't mean this life is easy. Sometimes my days seem booby-trapped with discouragement. And I believe one of Satan's biggest lies is this: "It's not going to be okay."

Buying into that lie causes us to question God's character, which can cripple our walk with Him and steal our focus. But our God is a miracle worker! All things are possible with Him. He saw "okay" and said, "I'll raise you eternal joy, a glorious inheritance, unconditional love, and freedom from worry." Thank You, Lord, for giving Your children better-than-okay lives.

JUST WAIT

Suzanne

Wait on the Lord: be of good courage, and he shall strengthen thine heart: wait, I say, on the Lord.
PSALM 27:14

Have you ever felt stuck? Like you're waiting for something to happen? It can make you feel antsy, restless, and anxious.

But waiting is a spiritual discipline that comes with a reward. Scripture says the Lord is good to those who wait on Him (Lamentations 3:25). There is comfort and growth to be found in that place of anticipation. So many times, I struggle to lay down my own timeline or submit to the Lord what I wish would happen and simply trust. But in that place of waiting—that is where the good stuff happens.

If you feel ready to move today but you're lacking wind in your sails, wait. Wait and see what God will do. Rest in His goodness, allow His Spirit to bring you comfort, and wait with great expectation of what He will do next. Be of good courage. Allow Him to strengthen your heart. His timing is always perfect.

DAILY CROSSES

Suzanne

*Then said Jesus unto his disciples, If any man
will come after me, let him deny himself,
and take up his cross, and follow me.*
MATTHEW 16:24

Sometimes obedience to Christ isn't easy. It doesn't
always feel good, nor is it always appealing. Sometimes taking the next step requires gritting your teeth, digging deep, and simply doing the thing you know He's asking you to do.

Jesus asks me to deny myself, take up my cross, and follow Him. Sounds tough. It's hard to deny myself and accept the burdens that may result. And yet when I feel that tug on my heart that I'm supposed to do something, the only thing that will bring me lasting peace and deep soul contentment is to yield. To take that step of obedience.

In the moment, it may not feel good, but in the big picture, obedience is the right path and the only way I will ever experience the joy that comes from an abiding relationship with my Savior. What cross is Jesus asking you to take up for His glory today? How can you submit more fully to Him?

CONVICTED CHRISTIAN

Carolyn

*For I am not ashamed of the gospel of Christ: for it
is the power of God unto salvation to every one that
believeth; to the Jew first, and also to the Greek.*

ROMANS 1:16

My dear sister in Christ, if you were on trial for your
faith, would you be convicted and declared guilty?
Is your faith bold and unwavering and so attractive to others that they want to know what gives you such love, joy,
and peace? I hope so!

Among all the people of the earth, how do people recognize us as Christians? Two unique marks of a Christ-follower that Jesus talked about are showing love (John
13:35) and bearing spiritual fruit (John 15:5). If we truly
belong to Christ, the gospel will fuel our love and our
works. Our focus on God's will and desires will increase,
and our focus on worldly passions and the enemy's distractions will decrease.

Be steadfast, then! Be alert and ready to share the gospel, even until your last breath. What glorious rewards
await the faithful believer!

Unfailing Love

Suzanne

---

*It is of the LORD's mercies that we are not
consumed, because his compassions fail not. They
are new every morning: great is thy faithfulness.*
LAMENTATIONS 3:22-23

These words from Lamentations were penned during
a true low point in Israel's history. Jerusalem lay in
ruins. As the prophet Jeremiah walked through its streets,
all he could see was pain, suffering, and destruction. I may
not have experienced destruction of this magnitude in my
life, but I certainly relate to the sense of grief and loss Jeremiah felt.

The prophet was well aware this wasn't the way things
were supposed to be. And yet he had hope. Why? Because
no matter how bad things get or how big we mess up or
disappoint others, God's mercy and love never fail. They
come to us freely, again and again like the morning's dawn.
In our darkest moments, God's love breaks through.

Rest in that truth today. His plans will prevail because
they are not dependent on you but on His character, His
faithfulness, His never-ending mercy, and His steadfast
love.

EYE ON THE PRIZE

Suzanne

*I press toward the mark for the prize of the
high calling of God in Christ Jesus.*
PHILIPPIANS 3:14

Many times at the start of the year, I have joined the gym with the intention of getting fit. On one such occasion, I decided to try a group exercise class that was quite challenging for me. Let's just say, I felt the fact that I hadn't worked out in a while.

That evening as I complained to my husband about my aching hip, he reminded me that the discomfort is natural. Anytime you push yourself to do something you're not used to doing, it's uncomfortable, even painful, at first. Think about waking up early to read your Bible, praying with your spouse, putting down your phone to interact, or showing hospitality.

I've regularly experienced the discomfort of pushing myself in these areas and others. But as I press toward the mark God has set before me, these actions become more natural, and I start to see results. So press on today, even if you know you're going to "feel it" later. That's progress you feel—the prize is coming.

A Fleeting Shadow

Carolyn

*Seeing his days are determined, the number
of his months are with thee, thou hast
appointed his bounds that he cannot pass.*
Job 14:5

For years, my youngest son carried guilt over his father's sudden death. My son normally would have been painting with his dad and the crew that sunny October day, but he had made other plans. After absorbing the shock of his dad's fatal heart attack while on the job, my son felt guilty. Maybe if he had been there, he thought, he could have saved his dad's life by doing CPR. Only recently did Scripture and our conversation help him heal.

Scripture reveals that life is short and fragile, like a fleeting shadow. God, who fearfully and wonderfully created us, knows us inside and out. He also knows our beginning and our end. Our days on Earth are determined and numbered by God, and no one can change His perfect plan.

If God wants you or me home with Him, no intervention will change that. CPR would not have changed God's plan that day. In fact, I see His mercy in shielding my son from witnessing his father's death and feeling helpless to save him. God has brought both of us healing as we've chosen to trust in His perfect plan.

SEEKING APPROVAL

Suzanne

> *For do I now persuade men, or God? or*
> *do I seek to please men? for if I yet pleased*
> *men, I should not be the servant of Christ.*
>
> GALATIANS 1:10

As a grown woman, I've been surprised at how often I am still affected by what others think of me (or what I think they're thinking). I can get so caught up in basing my value as a person entirely on how others treat me, if they notice me, or if they're pleased with me.

It seems even the apostle Paul wrestled with the approval trap: "Am I seeking the approval of God or man?" he asks.

It's a valid question. And the stakes are high. When I live to please others, I forfeit the opportunity to be a sold-out servant of Christ. I miss opportunities to do His bidding because I'm busy thinking about the opinions of others. When I seek to please God alone, I walk in the freedom and grace He intends. And the best part is, His approval can never be lost.

LOVE ONE ANOTHER

Suzanne

A new commandment I give unto you, That ye love one another; as I have loved you, that ye also love one another. By this shall all men know that ye are my disciples, if ye have love one to another.
JOHN 13:34-35

A few years ago, my sister snapped a frameable photo of my daughters, who were five and seven at the time. After a soccer game, my older daughter, Sadie, held her sister, Amelia, in a victory embrace. These are two passionate, opinionated girls who argue and disagree daily. But they also love each other fiercely. I think it's a pretty good picture of how love sometimes looks in the family of God.

Even though Scripture tells us that love is the distinguishing feature of a disciple, I don't always do it well. Too often I get caught up in differences of opinion, my own selfishness, and even pride. But these things should never override love.

Jesus, help me love my sisters and brothers well. Remind me that we are all part of Your family.

FRUIT OR FRUITS?

Carolyn

But the fruit of the Spirit is love, joy, peace,
longsuffering, gentleness, goodness, faith, meekness,
temperance: against such there is no law.
GALATIANS 5:22-23

I used to wonder why this passage says "the fruit of the
Spirit is" instead of "the fruit of the spirit *are*." Though
nine different virtues are listed, the verse seems to be
describing one fruit. A friend shared with me the analogy
of an orange. Though it is one fruit, it consists of many
individual sections joined together.

The Holy Spirit helps us develop Christian character. By surrendering to God's will and allowing the Spirit
to teach us, we can mature and experience a fruitful life.
Each virtue is worthy of attaining and needed to complete the Christian's character. As we grow in grace and
exhibit the whole fruit of the Spirit, our fleshly tendencies can be defeated.

Love, joy, and peace are from God. Longsuffering,
gentleness, and goodness are aimed toward others. And
faith, meekness, and temperance are for our own good. As
you cultivate the fruit of the Spirit, God will help you live
the abundant life He has for you.

BETTER THINKING

— *Suzanne* —

*Casting down imaginations, and every
high thing that exalteth itself against the
knowledge of God, and bringing into captivity
every thought to the obedience of Christ.*
2 CORINTHIANS 10:5

Do you ever feel weighed down by self-condemnation?
Maybe you allow worry to overwhelm you. Or perhaps you entertain bitter, envious, or prideful thoughts.
Too often I allow wrong thoughts to worm their way into
my mind and dictate how I feel and behave.

When I let my thoughts wander in the wrong direction, I waste time I could be using to love and serve. Wast-
ing this mental energy may seem harmless, but an off-track
thought life interferes with obedience. It can cause me to
be spiritually dull and miss opportunities.

Thriving in your walk with God begins with obedience in your thought life. When you feel your thoughts
veering down the wrong path—worry, self-doubt, envy,
bitterness, hatred—ask God to renew your mind (Romans
12:2). He will be faithful to do it. And as you replace faulty
thinking with truth, your thought life will be life-giving
and glorifying to God.

You Can Do It!

———— *Suzanne* ————

For God hath not given us the spirit of fear; but
of power, and of love, and of a sound mind.
2 Timothy 1:7

Since the time my thirdborn could speak, she has been proclaiming, "I can do it!"

When she was two, her older siblings would come to her to remove a twist-off lid or fix a broken toy. She's now seven, and just the other day, she offered to make me a cup of coffee using our instant-cup machine. I warned her that the cream container was too full, but she said boldly, "I can do it, Mom!" And she did.

I'm not sure where my daughter's sense of empowerment comes from, but as a child of God, I can live with similar confidence. God not only equips me for each task He calls me to—He also replaces my fear with power, love, and a sound mind.

As I depend on Him, I can confidently say, "I can do it!" regardless of my circumstances or the task at hand. I don't have to wonder if I am capable because I know where my strength and help come from.

A Christmas to Remember

Carolyn

*But Mary kept all these things, and
pondered them in her heart.*
Luke 2:19

Being in labor on Christmas Eve was an extraordinary experience. My husband, Randy, and I were hoping our first baby would arrive on Christmas Day and share a birthday with Jesus. Melissa Christine was born at 8:23 a.m. on Christmas morning and was later presented to us in a red Christmas stocking by the nursing staff. What a precious gift!

Our lives were forever changed when we became parents. Randy and I may have been separated from Joseph and Mary by nearly 2,000 years, but we undoubtedly shared the same wonder and emotions of being a father and mother for the first time. Challenged by the incredible responsibility and filled with a dimension of love we'd never felt before, we accepted the gift with awe and wonder.

Christmas will forever hold a special place in my heart, not only as the day of my Savior's birth, but also as the day I received one of my greatest gifts.

REAL BEAUTY

Suzanne

*Favor is deceitful, and beauty is vain: but a
woman that feareth the LORD, she shall be praised.*
PROVERBS 31:30

We live in a world that celebrates beauty and influence. As a woman, I can be tempted to believe being "beautiful" and being celebrated will make me feel more valuable. But when I've gone down that road, I've only realized how flawed I truly am.

My skin has blemishes, my teeth aren't sparkling white, and extra pounds stubbornly cling to my untoned body. If I was counting on my looks to make me feel significant, I would feel very unworthy. The good news is, the Bible says that my value as a woman isn't wrapped up in how I look or even the favor I receive from others. My worth is found in fearing the Lord, and true praise that lasts comes from Him.

There's nothing wrong with wanting to look outwardly appealing. God makes beautiful things! But as a woman, I also need to keep my quest for beauty in perspective. The most attractive things about me will always be those that flow from my relationship with God.

IN NEED OF REST

Suzanne

*Come unto me, all ye that labor and are
heavy laden, and I will give you rest.*
MATTHEW 11:28

Rest. We all need it, but it can be so elusive. We live in a world that measures our value by our accomplishments. Whether caring for my family, serving at church, or meeting deadlines for work, I feel pressure to do more and do it better. Busyness becomes a badge of honor as I think, *If I'm busy, I must be contributing.*

But God didn't design us to be contributing full-time. He offered His people, the Israelites, a day of rest—Sabbath.

In the New Testament, Jesus reiterated the idea of Sabbath when He invited all who are heavy laden to come to Him for rest. Sometimes that offer can seem implausible, and yet there it is. No matter how weary you are, God offers you rest today. No matter how burdened you are, He offers you respite. Slowing down can be difficult, but remember that you are designed for rest!

THE ART OF REARING CHILDREN

Carolyn

*Train up a child in the way he should go: and
when he is old, he will not depart from it.*
PROVERBS 22:6

I have read that you "raise" cattle, but you "rear" children. The meaning of the latter is to bring up a child in a specific manner until he is fully grown. The principles my husband and I based our parenting on were found in Scripture and demonstrated by Jesus's example.

As parents, we took joy in spending time with our children, building a strong and trusting relationship with them. During this precious time, we learned their interests and God-given talents and helped them pursue their strengths. We did our best to model a love for God's Word and respect for His authority in our lives. Though we were not perfect parents, we praised, encouraged, and disciplined our children with love.

Instilling reverence for the Lord has equipped our adult children to show respect and kindness to others and glorify God. I found the task of rearing our children to be a great privilege and responsibility. The season of child-rearing is temporary, but the fruit of parenting is eternal.

CHRIST PREACHED
IN EVERY WAY

Suzanne

*The one preach Christ of contention, not
sincerely, supposing to add affliction to my
bonds: but the other of love, knowing that
I am set for the defense of the gospel. What
then? notwithstanding, every way, whether in
pretense, or in truth, Christ is preached; and
I therein do rejoice, yea, and will rejoice.*
PHILIPPIANS 1:16-18

Preaching the gospel about Jesus is not always easy.
Whether disagreements in church or division over
politics, all the tension in the world can make our mission
feel impossible. But we don't have to do things perfectly
for the gospel of Jesus to break through and transform
lives.

Paul wrote the words of Philippians while he was
imprisoned. Even in that helpless place, he emphasized
that God uses imperfect people with imperfect motives to
spread Christ's messages of hope and restoration.

Where people are involved, there will always be messi-
ness. But I can trust Him to work through tense times and
imperfect people to accomplish His purposes. And I can
rejoice because in "every way," Christ is being preached.

A BETTER BODY

Suzanne

But now hath God set the members every one of
them in the body, as it hath pleased him. And if
they were all one member, where were the body?
But now are they many members, yet but one body.
1 CORINTHIANS 12:18-20

How well do you work with fellow believers? The apostle Paul compared the family of God, the church, to a physical body. Each person is like a different part of the body, but they are controlled by the same Spirit. This breaks down barriers, removes labels, and allows individuals who are extremely different from one another to have an amazing bond through faith in Christ.

We're meant to cooperate, not compete—each using the gifts God has given us. When we do, we participate in something beautiful and amazing. You are indispensable! And we can accomplish more together than we can apart.

Remember that truth today, and ask God how you can participate in His body in the ways He designed. He will reveal the specific roles and tasks He has prepared for you to do.

Coming Home

Carolyn

Grant thee according to thine own
heart, and fulfill all thy counsel.
PSALM 20:4

We're moving back home to be close to you."
My son's words brought tears to my eyes and filled my heart with gratitude. This news was a surprise to me, but not to God. After years of living in another state, my son and his wife were moving back to Ohio, to the town they'd grown up in. God had put all the pieces into place for them to do so.

My favorite translation of Psalm 20:4 says, "May he grant you your heart's desire and fulfill all your plans" (ESV). What a blessing that the Lord cares about the desires of our hearts. As I seek to submit my desires to His will for my life, I find that my plans naturally fall into harmony with His. And like the unexpected good news of my son's homecoming, God's perfect provision is often better than I could have imagined.

Urgent Soul Care

Suzanne

*He healeth the broken in heart, and
bindeth up their wounds.*
Psalm 147:3

It had been that kind of week. Everything seemed to go wrong. I was tired. I was stressed. I was emotionally low. I needed God's peace. Badly.

Sometimes I know I'm allowing the enemy to get a foothold—whether in parenting moments, during relationship struggles, or in permitting rogue lies to take root—but I feel powerless to stop it. I can lose sight of the goal, which is not for me to be happy and comfortable, but for God to be glorified through every thought, attitude, word, and action.

When I'm in that place, God can do such amazing things. And the best part is, He's right there with me. When I come to Him in bad shape, He performs triage and then manages my long-term soul care.

The coast is one of my favorite places to visit when I'm overwhelmed. A giant, pounding ocean is a great place to regain perspective. God's power is undeniable, and that powerful God is with you every step of the way.

UNDER CONSTRUCTION

Suzanne

This I say then, Walk in the Spirit, and
ye shall not fulfil the lust of the flesh.
GALATIANS 5:16

As a child, I sang a song that began, "He's still working on me, to make me what I ought to be…" Isn't that so true in life? As much as I'd like to believe I have this Christian life figured out, I find myself getting tripped up by stuff I should be past by now.

Paul talks about how the desires of the flesh go against the Spirit. The two are in constant opposition, and sin can keep us from doing the things we know are right. Jealousy, anger, idolatry, hatred, strife, and more unsavory characteristics threaten the work God wants to do in our lives.

In order to combat these ungodly tendencies, we must walk in the Spirit (verse 25). Then the fruit of the Spirit developing in our lives will crowd out everything else. Thank God today that He's still working on you, producing the fruit of righteousness as you walk with Him!

Darkness to Light

Carolyn

*Then spake Jesus again unto them, saying, I am the
light of the world: he that followeth me shall not
walk in darkness, but shall have the light of life.*

John 8:12

Many years ago, I went spelunking. What a fun adventure, exploring caves! We wore hats with headlamps and worked our way deep into the dark cave. Our leader guided our group into a large open area and directed us to turn off the lights on our hats.

Standing in total darkness was an unforgettable experience. Then our guide lit one candle, a single light in the midst of darkness. The light shone bright, illuminating the path forward.

Jesus conquered death and the darkness of sin through His resurrection. The "Light of the World" was forever victorious over His enemy, Satan. Because of that victory, our living Savior offers everlasting life to everyone who believes in Him. And as we draw near to the precious Giver of light, we will never walk in darkness.

GLORY IN WEAKNESS

Suzanne

*And he said unto me, My grace is sufficient for thee:
for my strength is made perfect in weakness. Most
gladly therefore will I rather glory in my infirmities,
that the power of Christ may rest upon me.*

2 CORINTHIANS 12:9

Nothing has shown me my weaknesses more than being a mom. Many days I feel like everyone's running in a different direction, testing my limits (and my sanity!). Being a mom is equal parts the thrill of victory and the agony of defeat—sometimes within the same five-minute span.

One minute I'm having a life-giving conversation with one of my kids, and the next I'm hiding out in the bathroom as he attempts to pound down the door. Even on hard days, I have no doubt God is still using me.

He is offering me grace and showing His power through my weakness. Whether you're mothering, dealing with the stress of a job, working on a tough relationship, or walking through a health challenge, God's grace is sufficient! You can glory in your weakness, knowing His mighty power rests on you.

Firm Plans

Suzanne

The counsel of the LORD standeth for ever, the
thoughts of his heart to all generations.
PSALM 33:11

A few years ago, I had the opportunity to visit Boston and see some of the historical sites. One such site was the Paul Revere House, where Revere and his family lived during the American Revolution. Built in 1680, it is the oldest home in Boston. Over 80 percent of the structure is original.

A building that has been standing for over three centuries is considered a marvel in this relatively young country. But how much more marvelous is it that the Lord's plans stand forever! When the world seems to be going crazy, we can take comfort that His purposes and heart for His people endure through all generations.

As I walked through the Paul Revere House with its creaky, slanted floors, I was reminded that unlike our human creations, God's workmanship doesn't degrade or decay. His plans and purposes hold fast, regardless of our external circumstances. In addition, His feelings for us never change.

Eternal Garden

— *Carolyn* —

And their soul shall be as a watered garden.
JEREMIAH 31:12

When a gardener plants a seed in his garden, he places it in the dark, moist soil. The seed develops roots that begin to stretch downward, looking for nutrients to satisfy its hunger. The roots stabilize the seed's position and provide sustenance.

Surrounded by the cold ground, the seed feels an incredible warmth penetrating its surroundings. Yearning for the source of the warmth, the seed stretches upward. It breaks through the surface into the sunlight, which produces the energy needed for growth.

Before the seed can become hot and dry, the gardener waters the garden, showering the soil and hydrating the thirsty seed. Growing is not easy. The seed may withstand floods, droughts, insects, pests, and weeds that want to strangle the very life out of it. It is the gardener's job to care for its every need. Finally, the seed fully matures into a plant that is pleasing to the eye and fulfills its purpose.

Are you planting seeds and cultivating souls? Are you growing under the care of the Master Gardener?

THE SADDEST VERSE

Suzanne

In those days there was no king in Israel, but every man did that which was right in his own eyes.

JUDGES 17:6

Someone once told me that Judges 17:6 was the saddest verse in the Bible. While there may be some other good candidates, I'm inclined to agree. Watching people completely abandon God's rule and give in to lawlessness is tragic to see. In truth, when we turn from God's Word and live according to our own desires, the results are devastating.

In our modern world, the urge to do what is right in our own eyes is stronger than ever. Moral absolutes have been abandoned in favor of doing what "feels right" and living "my truth." But relying on our own moral compasses, apart from God and His Spirit, leads to destruction.

Are you living in such a way that you're doing what is right in your own eyes? Don't make the same tragic mistake the Israelites did in the time of the judges. Living under Christ's authority is the only way to experience true freedom, hope, and peace.

Showing Hospitality

Suzanne

Use hospitality one to another without grudging.
1 Peter 4:9

My regular babysitter, Carol, is a great example of someone who shows hospitality. One day, I came home from work and she said, "Jeff dropped off that package."

"Jeff?" I asked.

"Your mailman," she replied. "Jeff."

I felt bad. I had seen a man putting letters in the metal boxes on an adjacent street, but I had never asked him his name.

Another day while Carol was on duty, a repairman came to fix our sink: "He told me about his one-week-old baby and showed me pictures!" she told me. "It was so cute!"

Scripture talks about hospitality being one of the marks of a Christian. Sometimes we may think about this characteristic as inviting someone over for dinner or to stay as a guest. But hospitality is also an attitude. We show hospitality when we make people feel welcome and valued. We show it when we slow down long enough to learn someone's name or ask them a question. Hospitality without grudging makes everyone feel invited in.

For Such a Time as This

Carolyn

*And who knoweth whether thou art come
to the kingdom for such a time as this?*
ESTHER 4:14

I have always been intrigued by the story of Esther, a young Jewish woman who lived in Persia during the exile of the Hebrews. After winning a beauty contest and becoming queen, Esther used her voice to bring about the deliverance of the Jews.

Before taking her bold step of faith, Esther fasted and prayed. Then she approached King Xerxes, setting aside the danger to herself to save her people. Because of Esther's bravery, Haman's evil plot to annihilate the Jews was unsuccessful.

In my lifetime, I may never be a heroine like Esther. But I can use my voice. Through conversations and writing, I seek to direct others' hearts and minds toward a thriving personal relationship with a loving God. When I feel my courage waning, that is when I pray for extra strength. How is God calling you to use your voice today? Don't be silent. God has you here "for such a time as this."

FULL COLOR

Suzanne

*But we are all as an unclean thing, and all
our righteousnesses are as filthy rags; and
we all do fade as a leaf; and our iniquities,
like the wind, have taken us away.*
Isaiah 64:6

One day, in the two-year-old classroom at church, the children busily colored a picture of Moses. Each child had her own plastic baggie of oversized crayons. Suddenly an outcry arose.

"Hey!" one little girl yelled. "This one doesn't work!"

I looked down to see that she was scribbling on the white coloring sheet with a white crayon. All the other children followed her lead, testing their own white crayons. The resulting uproar didn't cease until all the offending crayons had been collected.

It made me think of the times in life when I've been scribbling with a useless crayon. When have I depended on my own deeds to live a "good life"? Like coloring with those crayons, all my own good works are useless. Only Jesus can make me righteous before a holy and just God. When I trust in Him for my righteousness, my life is full of color and joy.

The Great Finisher

— Suzanne —

Being confident of this very thing, that he which hath begun a good work in you will perform it until the day of Jesus Christ.
PHILIPPIANS 1:6

Have you ever left a project unfinished? Maybe you started cleaning a room and got distracted halfway through the job. Perhaps you eagerly started a craft project but abandoned it long before it was complete. As people, we don't always finish what we start. But our God always does.

From the moment you accepted His free gift of salvation, He began doing a work in you, transforming you from glory to glory into the likeness of His Son, Jesus. The best part is, God is the One who does the work, not you. Today, He knows all that you will do and become, and He always finishes what He starts.

God will never give up on you or leave you to your own devices. He will continue to do His work in you today and all the days of your life.

Gentle Words

Carolyn

*A soft answer turneth away wrath: but
grievous words stir up anger.*
PROVERBS 15:1

Many years ago, I was working as a student nurse in surgery. All of a sudden, for a reason unbeknown to me, the surgeon in charge became angry and demanding. I responded to his gruff words with a soft and gentle voice. Immediately, I noticed a change in his demeanor. The tone of his voice shifted. The surgery continued with a calm that the entire surgical team could sense.

Words are powerful. They can build up or tear down. The Bible reminds us that our words should be well chosen, intended to nourish the souls of others. A gentle spirit will steer our conversations to a place that encourages, pacifies, and benefits others. Our responses should not be angry or harsh or intended to crush another's spirit.

Just as my response calmed the surgeon and his team, our soft words can bring peace to the anger and chaos around us. As we choose to be sensitive and disciplined in our responses, our words will edify others and draw them closer to God.

CHOSEN SERVANT

Suzanne

Ye are my witnesses, saith the LORD, and my servant whom I have chosen: that ye may know and believe me, and understand that I am he: before me there was no God formed, neither shall there be after me.
ISAIAH 43:10

Being a "witness" or telling another person about the gospel of Jesus can feel intimidating, but it doesn't have to be.

God has chosen us to represent Him to others that they might know Him, believe in Him, and understand that He is the one and only eternal God. Having spiritual conversations with others does just as much to strengthen our faith as it does to draw that person to God.

As I follow Christ, I provide a living, breathing example of who He is and how He has changed my life. Being a witness is simply responding to God's call to proclaim the difference He has made in my life and invite others to turn to Him and experience life. As God provides opportunities, I can be His witness, knowing that I am chosen by Him.

OPEN DOORS

Suzanne

*Furthermore, when I came to Troas to preach
Christ's gospel, and a door was opened unto me
of the Lord, I had no rest in my spirit, because I
found not Titus my brother: but taking my leave
of them, I went from thence into Macedonia.*
2 CORINTHIANS 2:12-13

Recently I made the mistake of comparing my own spiritual performance to that of the apostle Paul. "I'm sure Paul never rested from ministry to take some 'me time,'" I told a friend.

This woman challenged me with the story of Paul going to Troas. Though God opened an opportunity for him to preach there, Paul knew he wasn't up to it. He didn't walk through the door, which is almost shocking to this modern-day Christian.

Paul understood that freedom in Christ was true freedom and that God would do the work. If you're feeling burned out or spiritually depleted, remember that taking a "time-out" is okay. Paul went on to preach powerfully in other places once he was recharged. God always gives us what we need, and sometimes what we need is a break.

JESUS WEPT

Carolyn

Jesus wept.
JOHN 11:35

When my children were young, they attended a Christian school. Occasionally, one of them would come to me and say, "Mom, I have to memorize a Bible verse for school tomorrow." I often picked the shortest, easiest one in the Bible: "Jesus wept."

These two words are a beautiful expression of Jesus's humanity. Maintaining His divine nature, Jesus humbled Himself and walked in human shoes—or sandals, if we're being accurate.

John 11 recounts the death of Lazarus, a close friend of Jesus. Jesus arrives after Lazarus has died, and the man's sisters, Mary and Martha, tell Jesus if He had come sooner, their brother would be alive. As Jesus saw the women and others weeping, His spirit was deeply moved by their pain and grief.

He wept for His friends' suffering. He wept, knowing that moments later His words—"Lazarus, come forth"—would restore his friend's life and he would walk out of the grave. In two powerful words, our Savior showed His great love and compassion—Jesus wept.

LOVED BY DESIGN

Suzanne

I will praise thee; for I am fearfully and
wonderfully made: marvelous are thy works;
and that my soul knoweth right well.
PSALM 139:14

Whenever I'm feeling unsure of myself, I picture the little girl I once was. As a child, I was intensely creative and a bit weird. I was always making funny crafts, and one time, my brother and I attempted to build a horse barn out of scrap wood in our backyard. (It blew over in the first good wind.)

Back then, God already knew His purposes for me. He was shaping that little girl with all her quirks to do exactly what He had planned for her. At times, what I have to offer and even who I am may be rejected by people, but my design is intentional.

Pondering that truth flips my perspective. I am fearfully and wonderfully made. God loves me *and* likes me! When He saw that eccentric little girl, He already knew all the beautiful (and hard) things He had planned for her, and His purposes will not be thwarted. That melts away many of the rejections and hurts in this life.

Letting Go and Letting God

Suzanne

*To every thing there is a season, and a time to every
purpose under the heaven…a time to get, and a
time to lose; a time to keep, and a time to cast away.*
Ecclesiastes 3:1,6

Shortly after moving, I decided to purge. My daughter had a pair of boots that were terribly scuffed, so I tossed them in the kitchen trash can without a second thought.

A few hours later, I heard a wail coming from the kitchen. I raced downstairs to find my three-year-old clutching the discarded boots, crocodile tears running down her cheeks. Her toddler anguish was so cute, I snapped a few photos that make me smile to this day.

Do you ever find yourself struggling to let something go? Maybe it's a sweet season, or a relationship, or even a sentimental object you no longer need. The teacher in Ecclesiastes tells us that there is a time to keep and a time to cast away. This can comfort us in seasons of change. Is there something you need to let go of today? Place it in the capable hands of your Creator.

THE FIFTH COMMANDMENT

Carolyn

*Honor thy father and thy mother: that
thy days may be long upon the land
which the LORD thy God giveth thee.*
EXODUS 20:12

How is your relationship with your parents? Many find it difficult to honor parents who have criticized, abused, or abandoned them. Does God still expect us to honor parents who fail us? Yes, He commands it.

In the fifth commandment of ten, God expresses His design for the parent-child relationship. He offers an important rule for children: *Honor thy father and mother.* God is delighted when we obey this command. It allows Him to fulfill the promise of a blessed life for His children.

Parents deserve honor because of their God-given position; however, respect is earned through godly character and actions. Children are not required to respect parents who choose sin-sick lives, but they can pray for them and forgive. Obedience is not required when you are older and on your own, but honoring parents is always right in God's eyes. As we obey Him, God fulfills His promises in our lives.

GOD OF HOPE

Suzanne

Now the God of hope fill you with all joy and
peace in believing, that ye may abound in
hope, through the power of the Holy Ghost.
ROMANS 15:13

Have you ever had a bad day? Or maybe you had a bad week, month, or even year. Whether sickness, job stress, financial worries, or something else, the trials of this life can get us down.

When Paul traveled through the ancient world encouraging the Christian churches, he spoke to people who faced many struggles. The gospel of Jesus wasn't welcomed in that culture, and yet its power in the lives of believers was undeniable.

Paul encouraged the Christians to be filled with God's joy and peace through believing. He is bigger than every trial, and as we believe, He produces hope in our lives that is inexplicable apart from Him. If you're going through a time of discouragement, take a deep look at your faith and the One in whom you believe. He will fill you with joy, peace, and hope.

EMBRACING THE NEW

Suzanne

Behold, I will do a new thing; now it shall spring forth; shall ye not know it? I will even make a way in the wilderness, and rivers in the desert.
ISAIAH 43:19

Not long ago, I bagged up some clothes that were too small for my young son. Unfortunately, I wasn't stealthy enough, and he caught a glimpse of the bags and a favorite pair of pajamas he'd recently outgrown.

He ran to me with tears in his eyes. "I still want those!" he cried. I took him in my lap and explained that another little boy would get to enjoy his old clothes and that he had plenty of new clothes to wear.

I see a similar attitude in myself when it comes to allowing God to do new things in my life. Sometimes I cling to what has been because change is difficult for me. The unknown is scary. When life gets shaken up, I need to remember that God specializes in doing new things, and He has great intentions for those who follow Him.

MASTER TEACHER

Carolyn

Set your affection on things above,
not on things on the earth.
COLOSSIANS 3:2

I am part of the baby boomer generation. Growing up during the 1950s and '60s, my childhood memories of school include my Goldenrod ruled paper tablet, my jumbo box of crayons with a sharpener, and playing jump rope at recess with my friends.

At school, I learned the ABCs; reading, writing, and arithmetic; and other fundamentals that would help me grow and develop into a creative and intelligent person. If I obeyed the rules and did my lessons well, I would receive a good report card.

Since March 1971, when I accepted Christ as my Savior, I have been tutored by the Master Teacher. My curriculum comes from the Bible, and lessons include living by faith through trust and obedience to God, modeling a pure character with a servant's heart, and learning to depend on the Holy Spirit for wisdom and discernment.

As I learn from my Master Teacher, He focuses my mind on eternal goals and helps me grow in devotion to my Savior.

GLAD GIVER

— *Suzanne* —

Every man according as he purposeth in his heart, so let him give; not grudgingly, or of necessity: for God loveth a cheerful giver.
2 CORINTHIANS 9:7

I have a fear of the dentist's chair, especially when a drill is involved. So you can imagine my disappointment when I broke a dental crown just two years after its installment. To make matters worse, insurance refused to pay because the crown had failed so quickly. I told a few people about my plight and began planning how to pay for the unexpected expense.

One Saturday morning, shortly after my dental appointment, I noticed a card on the counter. Inside was a sweet handwritten note and a check for the exact amount of my procedure. My heart nearly exploded with gratefulness for the well-timed gift.

Maybe you've received a gift at just the right time. Or maybe you've had the joy of giving one. When we give of our resources, we please God, and He blesses us in return. The size of the gift doesn't matter as much as the attitude; we give gladly because He has given so much to us.

No Offense

Suzanne

The discretion of a man deferreth his anger;
and it is his glory to pass over a transgression.
PROVERBS 19:11

In the past few years, I've faced enough divisive issues to last me a lifetime. I've seen people be divided over politics, health choices, church decisions, and theological issues. Unity in the culture and the church seems to be at an all-time low, and people seem quick to take offense.

The Bible reveals that a wise person exercises patience and overlooks offenses. That can be hard to do when those around us are lashing out in anger and frustration. But glory comes from choosing *not* to get offended. I think glory is found in the fact that this action reflects God's grace. I was born offending Him and will continue to do so until I die. Yet because of Jesus, God chooses to overlook the offense, which is to His glory.

As I recognize His grace toward me in my transgressions, I will be more inclined to overlook the offenses of others, which brings glory to God.

MENTORING AT ALL AGES

Carolyn

Let no man despise thy youth; but be thou an
example of the believers, in word, in conversation,
in charity, in spirit, in faith, in purity.
1 TIMOTHY 4:12

One day my granddaughter sent me Bible verses hand-written in colorful markers and decorated with stickers. I was so encouraged by her beautiful artwork! Another day, an elderly saint known as "the card lady" sent me a card containing a sunflower (my favorite flower) bookmark to cheer my heart. My single friend inspired me to write down my thoughts on being a godly grandmother and share them with my family.

Whether you are a young girl, an elderly saint, a single woman, or someone else, *you* can make a difference in a fellow believer's life. Every Christian woman has a story to tell and gifts to use to reflect God's character and encourage others.

Encouraging, inspiring, and supporting someone as she grows in her faith can leave an indelible mark on her life. Be ready to minister and be ministered to—because mentors come in all ages.

BE OF GOOD CHEER

Suzanne

*These things I have spoken unto you, that
in me ye might have peace. In the world
ye shall have tribulation: but be of good
cheer; I have overcome the world.*
JOHN 16:33

Sometimes it seems like the world is full of bad news. Headlines, social media, and even our own personal struggles can convince us that there is little to be hopeful about in this life. Jesus challenged this notion when He told His disciples they would face tribulation. Following that declaration, He told them something that seemed counterintuitive: "Be of good cheer."

How can we be cheerful with all the bad news surrounding us? We can counteract it with the good news! Jesus tells us, "I have overcome the world." God the Son, who lived a sinless life, died a brutal death on the cross, rose from the grave three days later, and now advocates on our behalf to the Father (1 John 2:1) has already overcome this broken, sinful world. That is a reason to have hope and share that hope with others in all circumstances.

THE ADVOCATE

Suzanne

*My little children, these things write I unto you,
that ye sin not. And if any man sin, we have an
advocate with the Father, Jesus Christ the righteous.*
1 JOHN 2:1

When my oldest daughter was two, we took her to a local playground. She happily played in the toddler area until a four-year-old started telling her she couldn't use the slide. "You're too little," he said.

My husband, who is six feet eight, stood nearby as our toddler navigated this relational road bump. Not knowing what to do, Sadie finally told the boy, "Well...well... that's my dad!" She spun around, pointing at Kevin. That little boy didn't bother her again.

We also have an advocate. When the accuser tells us our sin is insurmountable, we can point to Jesus Christ, the One who redeemed us to righteousness. Through Him, the Father forgives all our transgressions, and we can approach Him freely. Turning from sin should always be a priority, but when we can't do it on our own, Jesus is our strong advocate.

EXCELLENT THINKING

--- *Carolyn* ---

Finally, brethren, whatsoever things are true,
whatsoever things are honest, whatsoever
things are just, whatsoever things are pure,
whatsoever things are lovely, whatsoever things
are of good report; if there be any virtue, and
if there be any praise, think on these things.
PHILIPPIANS 4:8

I don't think any of us would argue with the fact that what we think about influences our lives, speech, and actions. Guarding our thoughts is a daily challenge. We are in a battle, and our enemy, Satan, wants us to have negative, critical, and complaining attitudes.

As believers, God has given us His peace and power. We have the ability to use our minds for positive, careful, wise, and excellent thinking.

So how can we cultivate thoughts that are honest, pure, and lovely? And how can we protect our minds from deceitful, corrupt, and dishonorable thinking? We must guard our minds by living according to God's Word. As we meditate on Scripture and pray, God renews our minds to be more Christlike. Then the Spirit can guide our minds to right thinking.

ON THE MOVE

Suzanne

*And Jesus went about all the cities and villages,
teaching in their synagogues, and preaching
the gospel of the kingdom, and healing every
sickness and every disease among the people.*
MATTHEW 9:35

When we read about the ministry of Jesus, it's clear that He was constantly on the move. He didn't just go to the religious places and wait for people to come to Him. He went out into the cities and villages teaching, preaching, and healing. He *actively* addressed the needs of people "out there."

As I seek to emulate my Savior, I should evaluate how often I go out in my neighborhood and community. Am I actively seeking those who need to hear the gospel and receive my care? It's easy to get caught up in my own busy life and forget to engage with the people around me.

But God has commissioned me to be Jesus's hands and feet. Whether I'm at the store, a soccer game, or the coffee shop, opportunities to share Jesus abound. He's still on the move, and I want to move with Him.

HOPE FOR A TROUBLED HEART

Suzanne

*Let not your heart be troubled: ye
believe in God, believe also in me.*
JOHN 14:1

arrived at church with a heavy heart. Bad news in the
world along with turmoil in my own home had added
up to a feeling of hopelessness. During the worship service, tears began to spill out. I felt overwhelmed with the
heaviness of life.

God never intended for us to carry the weight of the
world on our shoulders. Alone, I am not strong enough to
absorb the sadness and disappointment I encounter in this
life. But Jesus told His disciples how to refocus their troubled hearts: remember the One in whom they believed.

This is what I must do when down days come, and
they will. I believe in God, the mighty Creator of the uni-
verse and Lover of my soul. I believe in Jesus, who will-
ingly went to the cross to pay the penalty for my sin and
give me eternal life. As I press into my belief, He lifts the
burden of my troubled heart.

JESUS IS COMING

—— *Carolyn* ——

Behold, I come quickly: blessed is he that keepeth
the sayings of the prophecy of this book.
REVELATION 22:7

Do you enjoy reading the ending of a book first? I don't. I love discovering the setting of a story and each distinctive character. I enjoy seeing the theme emerge as the story unfolds. For me, reading the book is a journey that engages my imagination and allows me to expect the ending, whether I am right or wrong.

I have read the Bible from Genesis to Revelation, and I know the glorious ending. My Savior, Jesus Christ, is coming back! All of Scripture reveals His wonderful story from the beginning of time to His future return. Jesus fulfilled hundreds of prophecies by coming to Earth, living a sinless life, dying on the cross, and rising again. As believers, we must stay alert and keep our eyes focused upward, waiting with great joy and anticipation for Jesus's return and our promised eternal heavenly home.

WATCHING MY WORD COUNT

Suzanne

*In the multitude of words there wanteth not
sin: but he that refraineth his lips is wise.*
PROVERBS 10:19

The moment the words left my mouth, I knew I'd said
too much. What had started as a friendly chat with a
friend had drifted into gossip and speculation. I thought
of an object lesson I saw as a kid. It involves a tube of
toothpaste. Like our words, the teacher explained, the
paste easily comes out of the tube. However, once it's out,
there's no way to put it back in.

Undoing my sinful words would require confession,
repentance, and an apology when I would have been better off if I just held my tongue! Scripture tells us that in the
presence of many words, there is great opportunity for sin.
That doesn't mean we can't have in-depth conversations.
But when we get talking, we do need to be on the alert to
be sure the enemy isn't getting a win. And when in doubt,
not saying anything can be a wise move.

Transformational
Thanksgiving

Suzanne

Oh that men would praise the LORD for his
goodness, and for his wonderful works to the
children of men! For he satisfieth the longing
soul, and filleth the hungry soul with goodness.
PSALM 107:8-9

My young children don't always remember to thank me. So when they take the time to genuinely show gratitude for something I've done for them, my heart nearly explodes with joy. I wonder if God feels the same way when we, His children, thank Him for who He is and what He's done.

When I reflect on God's character and consider His works, thankfulness is a natural response. He is good. His love is steadfast. He does wondrous works for us, satisfies our deepest longings, and fills our hungry souls with good things. Even if God was all we had, there is so much to be thankful for!

As I make thanksgiving a habit in my life, I'm able to see God's glory more fully and proclaim His love and goodness to others. What can you thank the Lord for today?

CHANGING WORLD, UNCHANGING GOD

Carolyn

For I am the LORD, I change not.
MALACHI 3:6

Have you ever seen a chameleon? Its most unique feature is its ability to change its skin color, allowing the reptile to blend in with its habitat. Our Lord's handiwork is also seen when a caterpillar changes into a beautiful butterfly. As humans, we start out as helpless infants and grow into children and then adults. We change in many ways throughout our lives. God's purpose in this change is intentional and beneficial for His creation.

In contrast, God Himself is unchanging. He is the same "yesterday, today and forever" (Hebrews 13:8). What comforting words for the believer! The Lord is faithful with unfailing compassion, mercy, grace, and love. His redemption of us through Jesus is complete. We can have faith in His promises, which stand forever, from generation to generation. His presence and peace endure.

We are witnesses to our unchangeable Lord. Our families, friends, and coworkers need to hear about our faithful God. May we be quick to share the hope we have in an ever-changing world.

WHAT DID I DO WRONG?

Suzanne

Search me, O God, and know my heart:
try me, and know my thoughts: and see
if there be any wicked way in me, and
lead me in the way everlasting.
PSALM 139:23-24

One day I disciplined my young son for having a tantrum and tossing a full cup of water out of the bathtub in the process. After he'd gotten dressed and calmed down, he sat down beside me, his lip still quivering.

"What did I do wrong?" he asked, penitence in his voice.

I put my arms around him and explained that tantrums and throwing water were not acceptable behaviors. I told him I loved him and all he needed to do was say, "I'm sorry." He did, I forgave him, and we embraced.

Because my flesh is opposed to the ways of God, sometimes I'm blind to my many transgressions. Like the psalmist, I can ask God to reveal sin in my life so I can turn from it and walk in His way. When I do, God delights in offering forgiveness and restoring our relationship.

CLEAN HANDS, PURE HEART

Suzanne

*Who shall ascend into the hill of the LORD? or who
shall stand in his holy place? He that hath clean
hands, and a pure heart; who hath not lifted
up his soul unto vanity, nor sworn deceitfully.*

PSALM 24:3-4

Who has a right relationship with God? This passage answers that question: the one with clean hands and a pure heart. A pure heart comes from trusting Jesus to cleanse us from all sin and make our hearts new; clean hands follow. The things I choose to do and get involved in reveal the state of my heart.

We will lift our souls to the things we value. Many things can steal our attention away from God—our families, work, relationships, the media we consume, and even our own opinions. God wants to be number one in our lives. He is infinitely deserving of that position. What do you "lift up your soul" to? When you make God and His ways your first priority, you will be better able to enjoy the feeling of His presence.

Loving Our Own

Carolyn

*Let love be without dissimulation. Abhor that
which is evil; cleave to that which is good. Be
kindly affectioned one to another with brotherly
love; in honor preferring one another.*
ROMANS 12:9-10

I have always loved the acronym JOY as a reminder of relationship priorities:

Jesus Others You

Jesus first, others second, and yourself last. Attending to our own interests comes fairly naturally, and we cultivate passion for Jesus through prayer and reading His Word. But learning to love others deferentially can be difficult.

The New Testament provides many instructions about how to love one another. Our love should be sincere and abounding, marked with tolerance and kindness. Sometimes it means speaking the truth in love, overlooking an offense, confessing sin, or choosing to forgive. As we pursue Christlike fellowship with our brethren, we provide an example to unbelievers of God's extravagant, inclusive, sacrificial love. As we love one another, the world can see Him more clearly.

HEART HEALTH

— *Suzanne* —

*Keep thy heart with all diligence; for
out of it are the issues of life.*
PROVERBS 4:23

A s I walked out of the theater at the end of the movie,
I knew I should have left earlier. Within the first
few minutes of the film, I sensed the content was at odds
with my beliefs and standards. But I'd paid the ten-dollar
admission, so I waited it out, hoping it would get better. It didn't.

Maybe you've had a similar experience. A movie, book,
or conversation left you feeling like there was a layer of
sludge covering your heart. The word "heart" is men-
tioned nearly 900 times in Scripture. No wonder Proverbs warns that we must diligently guard it! Everything in
life—our emotions, words, and actions—proceeds from
the heart.

We must keep our hearts free from sin, toxic relationships, and anything else that makes them sick. Be wise
about the people and influences you allow into your life.
When your heart is healthy, other parts of your life will
be healthy too.

FAITH OVER FEAR

Suzanne

There is no fear in love; but perfect love casteth out fear: because fear hath torment. He that feareth is not made perfect in love.

1 JOHN 4:18

When I was in college, I developed a debilitating autoimmune condition seemingly overnight. It took several years to get to the bottom of what was causing the illness and recover (I'm grateful I did). At the onset—as I considered dropping out of college—fear plagued me.

Getting through that difficult time was a journey of learning to trust in God's love. Though I was barely getting through each day, I had to release fears and "what ifs," knowing that God was with me and had a good plan for my life.

In recent years, I've found many opportunities to give in to fear, including a child's health issues and special needs, current events, and even a global pandemic. Learning to release my worry and be filled with God's love has been a process. Anxiety still rears its ugly head. But as I focus on the enormity of God's love, I find my fear fading away.

A Glad Heart

Carolyn

A merry heart maketh a cheerful countenance.
PROVERBS 15:13

I am a people watcher when I am out and about. I study hairstyles, clothing trends, and faces. One of the nicest things to see is a smile on someone's face. When I see them smile at me, I smile back. There is a connection between us. Smiling can be contagious. It can be just what it takes to make someone's day and encourage their heart.

Only the Lord truly knows your heart. He is the source of all joy and gladness that we experience. But your countenance reveals what your heart feels. If someone has gladness in her heart and is content and satisfied with her life, she will have a radiant countenance.

Psalm 4:6 says, "There be many that say, Who will show us any good? LORD, lift thou up the light of thy countenance upon us." Try praying this simple prayer today: *Dear Lord, please allow Your goodness, gladness, and light to be reflected in my cheerful countenance.*

God's Help Desk

Suzanne

God is our refuge and strength, a
very present help in trouble.
PSALM 46:1

One day I took my car to the auto shop because it
had been acting up. As I sat in the waiting room, I
listened in as a mechanic at the front desk fielded half a
dozen phone calls. He seemed familiar with each vehicle, patiently asked questions, and expertly (and quickly!)
offered a solution. Each call lasted only minutes.

When things are going wrong with my car, taking it to
an expert who can diagnose and fix the problem is a relief.
And when things are going wrong in my life, the Expert
of *all things* is right there to assist me.

Like that mechanic, God listens to my problems—
even though He's already intimately acquainted with
them—strengthens me, and offers immediate help with
my troubles. What a reassuring truth! God's help desk is
open 24/7. He's waiting for me to come to Him with my
problems because He has all the solutions.

LIVING FOR NUMBER ONE

Suzanne

I am crucified with Christ: nevertheless I live; yet not I, but Christ liveth in me: and the life which I now live in the flesh I live by the faith of the Son of God, who loved me, and gave himself for me.

GALATIANS 2:20

When I was a child, my mom would sometimes chastise me with the phrase "You were looking out for number one." This meant I had made a decision based solely on what *I* wanted without considering the thoughts and feelings of others.

I still have more moments than I'd care to admit where I look out for number one. But as a believer, I am called *not* to live for myself but to live for Christ. His love and redemption motivate me to put to death my own agenda and desires and live fully for Him. The Holy Spirit helps me do this daily as I lay down my life and allow Christ to live in me. Only then can I live for the real Number One, my Lord and Savior Jesus Christ.

ONENESS IN JESUS

Carolyn

*There is neither Jew not Greek, there is
neither bond nor free, there is neither male
or female: for ye are all one in Christ Jesus.*
GALATIANS 3:28

In my home, I have a framed panoramic view of Jerusalem. It is a beautiful reminder of my trip to the Holy Land, where I experienced the sounds, sites, and smells of the historic nation of Israel. I was fascinated by the diverse sects within the Jewish community and also with the various Gentiles who live and work there. The common bond for the messianic (believing) Jews and the Christian Gentiles is faith in Jesus.

The apostle Paul spoke of the Jews and their rejection of the gospel of Christ (Romans 11). Because of the Jews' disobedience and unbelief, the Gentiles, through their faith and God's grace, were given the opportunity to be grafted into the glorious family of God. Neither racial descent, social status, sex, nor spiritual worthiness prevents a person from having saving faith in Christ. All believers are spiritually blessed and equal heirs because they are one in Christ. Rejoice!

HIS EYE IS ON THE SPARROW

Suzanne

*Behold the fowls of the air: for they sow not, neither
do they reap, nor gather into barns; yet your heavenly
Father feedeth them. Are ye not much better than they?*
MATTHEW 6:26

When my son was in the hospital for ten days with an unknown illness, "His Eye Is on the Sparrow," a song by Civilla D. Martin, brought me great comfort.

> Why should I feel discouraged,
>   why should the shadows come,
> Why should my heart be lonely,
>   and long for heav'n and home,
> When Jesus is my portion?
>   My constant Friend is He:
> His eye is on the sparrow,
>   and I know He watches me.

Knowing that God cares for even the sparrow reminds me that His love and care for me is greater than I can imagine. He sees every pain and insurmountable situation and tends to my deepest needs. When my son was in the hospital with an unknown future, God already knew the many ways He would provide and bring Himself glory. Whatever pain you're facing, God sees you and will provide all you need for today.

Growing Up

Suzanne

---

*That we henceforth be no more children, tossed
to and fro, and carried about with every wind
of doctrine, by the sleight of men, and cunning
craftiness, whereby they lie in wait to deceive; but
speaking the truth in love, may grow up into him
in all things, which is the head, even Christ.*

Ephesians 4:14-15

Ever since I left my parents' home, there are certain
things that make me feel like a "real" adult—making
a doctor's appointment, paying bills, getting an oil change.
As a youth, these were tasks I associated with adulthood,
and now, whenever I do them, I feel like I'm a true adult.

In Ephesians, Paul talks about what it looks like to
grow into spiritual adulthood. One mark of maturity is a
steady faith that resists false doctrine and the latest craze.
Another mark of growth is mature communication. Not
only is the Christian to speak truth, but she must do it in
love—in order to "grow up" into Christ.

When you think of being a spiritual adult, what attributes
come to mind? Possessing a firm faith, grounded in
truth and love, is a good place to start.

PRAYER WARRIORS

Carolyn

*Confess your faults one to another, and pray one
for another, that ye may be healed. The effectual
fervent prayer of a righteous man availeth much.*
JAMES 5:16

Prayer is powerful! We often resort to prayer after our
own methods are thwarted. If we had entrusted our
needs to the source of power first, our requests would have
been heard and cared for by the Omnipotent Father in
His perfect will and timing.

I have three dear friends who encourage and support
me in prayer. We sometimes pray together in person, but
we often pray spontaneously on the phone when one of
us has a need or spiritual concern. Our bond as sisters in
Christ has strengthened because we are empowered prayer
warriors for one another.

Our prayers reach the ears of our Father, and they
availeth much! He knows our hearts and our thoughts,
but He desires that we humble ourselves and pray in
dependence on Him. When the words won't come, the
Holy Spirit intercedes for us. So whether you kneel or
stand, remember to pray with faith anytime, anywhere,
and always.

FUTURE GLORY

Suzanne

---

*For I reckon that the sufferings of this present
time are not worthy to be compared with
the glory which shall be revealed in us.*

ROMANS 8:18

My daughter stared at the computer screen as a tear slipped silently down her cheek. The test question before her seemed insurmountable, and she felt the frustration of not knowing the answer. As her parent, I had compassion for her predicament. I also knew that getting one question wrong (or even a whole test) would not ruin her life or destroy her academic career.

In the Christian life, testing comes. In the midst of those trials, I can feel like my daughter—discouraged and hopeless. My heavenly Father not only has compassion for me, but He also has a glorious future in mind. In fact, that future is so great that the sufferings of this life are not even in the same category!

When I'm staring at that computer screen, frustrated and uncertain, I can remind myself that the pain of the test is temporary. One day, suffering will melt away as God reveals His glory in me.

HIGHER WAYS

Suzanne

*For my thoughts are not your thoughts,
neither are your ways my ways, saith the
LORD. For as the heavens are higher than
the earth, so are my ways higher than your
ways, and my thoughts than your thoughts.*
ISAIAH 55:8-9

Have you suffered a major disappointment or heartbreak? In those moments, God can feel very far away. We struggle to understand why God would allow it. We may even want to blame Him for not changing the circumstances.

Not long ago, I heard a young woman talk about losing her brother in a car accident. "I realized it wouldn't do me any good to blame God," she said, "especially because I needed Him more than ever."

When bad things happen, it's natural to question God's plan. When Job lost his children, he asked God some tough questions. God answered by showing Job his mental limitations in light of divine wisdom. A man could never understand the thoughts and actions of an omniscient, omnipotent God. The truth that remains is that God is love. And when life doesn't make sense, we can trust He is still working.

A Personal Reflection
on Psalm 23

Carolyn

The LORD is my shepherd; I shall not want.
PSALM 23:1

Have you ever put a meaningful Scripture passage into your own words? During a difficult season, I did this with Psalm 23:

The Lord and Savior is my caretaker. I will not need or desire anything He has not already provided for me. He gives me opportunities to rest in the busyness of life. He carries my burdens and offers moments of complete peace. My body is refreshed, and my spiritual soul is renewed. He guides me so my actions and thoughts align with His will and honor His name.

Even though I know my journey on Earth is short and death is an absolute, I am not afraid because my Savior promises to never leave me. I acknowledge His authority, protection, deliverance, support, and comfort.

My Lord, and my friend, is preparing a glorious banquet. Although I am unworthy, He honors me by anointing my head with oil. I embrace the assurance of His goodness and mercy during my earthly life while joyfully anticipating my future heavenly home with Him.

CHANGED BY LOVE

Suzanne

But after that the kindness and love of God our Savior toward man appeared, not by works of righteousness which we have done, but according to his mercy he saved us, by the washing of regeneration, and renewing of the Holy Ghost.
TITUS 3:4-5

Sometimes my heart is heavy about the things going on in the world. I know I am called to love others, and yet I am a broken, imperfect person who often fails. I see plainly how much there is to "fix" and how powerless I am to fix it. Many days it feels like hate is winning.

There's a reason for that feeling of powerlessness. One well-meaning person cannot correct all that is wrong with the world. Even a large group of well-meaning people can't do that. Only a kind, merciful, and righteous God can affect the heart change needed to replace hate with love.

And I have a part to play. As my heart is changed by the Holy Spirit, God's love can grow in my life and spread to those around me.

Tell Your Story

Suzanne

*My mouth shall show forth thy righteousness
and thy salvation all the day; for I know not
the numbers thereof. I will go in the strength
of the Lord GOD: I will make mention of
thy righteousness, even of thine only.*
PSALM 71:15-16

Not long ago, I had the opportunity to help tell the story of a ninety-four-year-old Black minister from California. I was fascinated by the stories of his youth—serving in the navy, marrying his sweetheart, raising six daughters, and leading a large congregation. His experiences were very different from my own, and yet God's greatness was evident in each one.

We need to hear one another's stories. You and I may have very different experiences and backgrounds, but we are united through Christ! I loved how the preacher's grandson, with whom I was working, referred to me as "sister."

Sister, you need to proclaim God's righteousness and the ways He has rescued you and intervened in your life! As we share our stories, we give testimony to God's faithfulness. And our story has the power to encourage others.

RESURRECTION JOY

Carolyn

He is not here, but is risen!
LUKE 24:6

An Easter tradition I enjoy with my grandchildren is making resurrection rolls. We dip a marshmallow in oil, roll it in a combination of sugar and cinnamon, wrap it in a crescent roll, and bake it in the oven. When we take the roll out, the marshmallow has melted, which leaves the roll "empty." Delicious!

As we do this project together, we talk about the Easter story. After Jesus was crucified, His body was removed from the cross. It was prepared with anointing oil and spices by Nicodemus, a Pharisee. He and Joseph of Arimathea, who owned the tomb, wrapped the body of Jesus in linen cloths. He was laid in the tomb, and a large, heavy stone was rolled in front.

On Easter morning, when some women came to the tomb to anoint Jesus's body with more spices, they became the first eyewitnesses to the empty tomb. Jesus was not there; He had risen! What great joy for all believers. Reminding my grandchildren of these precious things invites them into the celebration for our living Savior.

Going Home

Suzanne

> *For we know that if our earthly house of*
> *this tabernacle were dissolved, we have a*
> *building of God, an house not made with*
> *hands, eternal in the heavens. For in this we*
> *groan, earnestly desiring to be clothed upon*
> *with our house which is from heaven.*
> 2 CORINTHIANS 5:1-2

There's just something about "going home." College kids bring bags of laundry home for long weekends. Thousands of people migrate to their places of origin around the holidays. Many others return home to care for aging parents or recuperate during a difficult season.

There is something freeing about going home. There's no pretense because people there know you. When I return to my parents' house, I immediately feel comfortable and comforted by familiar sights, sounds, and smells.

Scripture tells us that this world is not our home. Part of the struggle of living is having a deep, gut-level desire to be in our eternal home, where every wrong is righted and every tear is wiped away. What a comfort that at the end of life here on Earth, God offers us *home* and eternal joy in His presence.

INSPIRING BEAUTY

Suzanne

*For thus saith the LORD that created the
heavens; God himself that formed the earth
and made it; he hath established it, he created
it not in vain, he formed it to be inhabited:
I am the LORD; and there is none else.*

ISAIAH 45:18

Not long ago, a friend and I visited Yosemite National Park. As we took in the beauty of waterfalls, towering walls of granite, and giant sequoias, we were filled with the wonder of God. He had made these incredible things on purpose—for His glory and also for us to enjoy.

At Tunnel View, one of Yosemite's most famous views, we stared in awe at El Capitan and Bridalveil Falls. Half Dome rose up in the background. My friend and I were nearly speechless until she said, "Thank You, Jesus. Thank You for making this."

Natural beauty like that of Yosemite inspires us and turns our thoughts to a wise and intentional Creator. It reminds us that He is the Lord and there is no one like Him. When our problems seem large, we can remember the wonders our God has created and His massive love for us.

MIRROR REFLECTION

Carolyn

---

*For if any be a hearer of the word, and
not a doer, he is like a man beholding his
natural face in a glass: for he beholdeth
himself, and goeth his way, and straightway
forgetteth what manner of man he was.*
JAMES 1:23-24

As you get older, it seems like time flies (in Latin, *tempus fugit*). Looking in the mirror, I see a woman with wrinkles, shrinking clothes, glasses, and a need for the TV volume to be higher. My husband's grandmother used to say, "I am as old as my tongue and a little older than my teeth." Alas, the natural bodily changes are plainly revealed in the mirror. And when I walk away, it's hard to forget what I look like.

Aging has motivated me to crave a more intimate communion with God. In the stillness of the early mornings, I find myself seeking direction from the whispers of His voice and the wisdom of His written Word. I desire to know Him more and to delight to be a doer of His Word, for this is what it means to live my whole life for Him.

Just Wait

Suzanne

*I wait for the LORD, my soul doth
wait, and in his word do I hope.*
PSALM 130:5

Sometimes waiting is hard. Waiting for a new job to start. Waiting for a baby to be born. Waiting to meet someone or get married. Life is full of waiting. Personally, I love feeling like I'm in control and don't have to wait. But when I impatiently rush ahead, I can become weary and experience feelings of burnout.

God offers another way. He invites us to wait on Him and hope in His Word. As we do, He recharges us and prepares us for the task ahead. Only He can provide the supernatural stamina we need to accomplish the good works He has planned for us.

When the daily grind saps your energy or the demands of life threaten to overwhelm you, wait. Wait on the Lord. Hope in His Word. He will calm your soul and give you exactly what you need to take the next step.

BE OF GOOD COURAGE

Suzanne

*Have not I commanded thee? Be strong and
of a good courage; be not afraid, neither
be thou dismayed: for the LORD thy God
is with thee whithersoever thou goest.*
JOSHUA 1:9

Courage comes in many forms. Sometimes we need the courage to speak truth in a tense conversation. Other times we must bravely take action when no one else will. Still other times we may need to face an intimidating situation.

As believers, we have Someone who goes with us into every grave circumstance and hard conversation. He emboldens us to follow His commands, do what is right, and overcome our fear.

When God led Joshua and the Israelites into the land He had promised them, they had many fears. They would need to overtake fortified cities and fight giants. From a human perspective, their chances of success did not look good. But God commanded Joshua and the people to be strong and have courage because He was with them. We serve the same God. As His daughters, we can have full confidence in Him, even when life gets scary.

FIRST LOVE

Carolyn

He must increase, but I must decrease.
JOHN 3:30

Do you remember the joy you experienced when you first asked Jesus into your heart and you knew the Holy Spirit was with you, guiding and teaching you God's truth? This beautiful relationship with a triune God was to become your "first love."

I encourage you to make your life count for God. One way to express your love for Him is by sharing your faith through your personal testimony. No one can refute your story of how you came to know the Lord Jesus as your Savior. The apostle Paul's extraordinary conversion from being a persecutor of Christians to a defender of the church and the gospel demonstrates the transforming power of Jesus. Paul humbled himself to give the rightful honor to Jesus.

John the Baptist, who proclaimed that Jesus was the Messiah, declared his unworthiness to even untie Jesus's sandal. He witnessed the glory of Christ increasing even as his popularity decreased. This was God's plan. Until the day you see your first love face-to-face, share your faith so that others may know Him.

SOLID ROCK

Suzanne

*Therefore whosoever heareth these sayings of
mine, and doeth them, I will liken him unto a
wise man, which built his house upon a rock.*
MATTHEW 7:24

Growing up, "The Solid Rock" was one of my favorite hymns. On Sunday mornings, we would lift our voices in the great old song:

> My hope is built on nothing less than Jesus's blood
> and righteousness. I dare not trust the sweetest
> frame, but wholly trust in Jesus's name. On Christ
> the solid Rock I stand, all other ground is sinking
> sand. All other ground is sinking sand.

Jesus is a solid Rock. But through His teaching, our Savior reveals that *knowing* He is a firm foundation and *doing* something about it are two different things. I know that the most secure way to live my life is by doing God's will, but unless I actually do it, I stand on unstable ground.

Are you standing on the solid Rock today? What might change if you put into practice the sayings of Jesus to love others, seek peace, live in humility, and pursue righteousness? Jesus is a solid Rock in a world of sinking sand.

SEASONS

— *Carolyn* —

*And he said unto them, It is not for you
to know the times or the seasons, which
the Father hath put in his own power.*
ACTS 1:7

Through my spiritual journey, I have not only experienced many seasons of life; I have also become a seasoned believer. I consider my salvation as a young woman to be the "spring" of my life. I married my high school sweetheart, I began my career as a nurse, and we started raising our three children. This was the "summer" of my life.

We all grew older in age and in our faith, experiencing high school and college graduations, marriages, and six wonderful grandchildren. Medical challenges crept in, and my husband, the patriarch, went to be with the Lord, culminating in the "fall" of my life.

I am currently in the "winter" of my life, as I face this journey as a widow and orphan. I am reminded daily of God's presence, provision, protection, and deep love for me. I fully trust in Him. Through joy, heartache, and big changes, God is intimately aware of the seasons of our lives. He remains the same through every transition.

CHANGE OF HEART

Suzanne

Let him that stole steal no more: but rather let him labor, working with his hands the thing which is good, that he may have to give to him that needeth.
EPHESIANS 4:28

almost didn't see the man standing on the corner. "Look, Mom!" my seven-year-old blurted.

A glance at the sign he held revealed the man needed money for his family, who sat nearby. I wasn't planning to turn around, but my children were insistent. "I want to go home and get my dollars," my daughter said.

I had a few small bills, so we turned around. But when we returned to the corner, the family was gone. We prayed as we drove slowly through nearby parking lots. Suddenly, we came across another family holding a sign. I saw an opportunity for my children to do what God had placed on their hearts, so I pulled over. My son handed six dollars through the open window.

"Thank you!" the man said. "God bless your children!"

My kids' compassionate response reminded me that I am instructed to give to those in need. I plan to be ready next time.

LITTLE GIFTS

Suzanne

*Every good gift and every perfect gift is from above,
and cometh down from the Father of lights, with
whom is no variableness, neither shadow of turning.*
JAMES 1:17

My son, Josiah, has a special appreciation for life. He's the first to proclaim "That's amazing!" when a school bus drives through the neighborhood or I make him his favorite meal.

One time we were walking from our hotel to spend a day at a theme park. "Can we ride the shuttle bus?" Josiah asked.

I explained that we had not bought tickets and would have to walk. All of a sudden, a bus pulled beside us, and the driver waved us over. "We're giving free rides today," she said.

"Wow!" Josiah exclaimed. "That's amazing!"

It was a great reminder to me of the many amazing gifts God gives us each day. So many times, I don't pause to notice His generosity in a serendipitous conversation or an unexpected blessing. Josiah's enthusiasm for life is a great reminder to enjoy God's little gifts and praise Him.

Spiritual Fitness

Carolyn

*And the brethren immediately sent away
Paul and Silas by night unto Berea: who
coming thither went into the synagogue of
the Jews. These were more noble than those
in Thessalonica, in that they received the word
with all readiness of mind, and searched the
scriptures daily, whether those things were so.*
ACTS 17:10-11

The Bereans were a group of people who were praised for searching the Scriptures daily to discern if what Paul and Silas preached was true. I love studying the Bible with other believers who treasure the wisdom, knowledge, and understanding within its pages. Being familiar with and memorizing God's Word allows me to easily identify false doctrine. It is also practical for knowing how I should live.

Spiritual fitness requires a working knowledge of God's Word. The goal is to be prepared to share the gospel message with others while exercising a servant's heart. We often set goals for physical fitness through nutrition and exercise. But we can be spiritually fruitful by feasting on the truth of Scripture and exercising the principles we find.

GOOD THOUGHTS

Suzanne

For I know the thoughts that I think toward
you, saith the LORD, thoughts of peace, and
not of evil, to give you an expected end.
JEREMIAH 29:11

What do I expect from God? If I look at how Scripture reveals His character, I expect Him to be good, loving, just, merciful, faithful, and kind. But sometimes I have trouble aligning what I expect from God with the circumstances in my life. I may wonder why a loved one passes away unexpectedly or why I struggle with a health crisis.

In the midst of exile, the Israelites must have wondered if what they were experiencing was really God's plan. Away from home and country, a low point in their history, they may have felt forgotten by God. But through the prophet Jeremiah, God reminds them that His thoughts for them remain firm. These thoughts are of peace, not of evil. They can expect that God's good plan for them will work out in the end.

When God seems silent or when I don't understand His ways, I can lean into the truth that His promises never change and His thoughts for me are for my good. I can expect to see great things.

A Prayer Away

Suzanne

*Then shall ye call upon me, and ye shall go and
pray unto me, and I will hearken unto you.*
JEREMIAH 29:12

Just past Jeremiah 29:11—one of the most quoted
verses in the Bible—we find another gem of a verse.
Not only does God have good thoughts and plans for His
people, but He hears our prayers! What a comfort that we
can call upon the Lord at any time and He will respond.

In times of peace and joy, God is listening. In times of
turmoil and grief, God is listening. No matter your situation, His Word promises that when you cry out to Him,
He hears and responds.

What do you need to talk to God about today? Even
though He is mighty and powerful, He is also personal.
He knows everything going on in your life, and He desires
to draw near to you as you draw near to Him in prayer.
Don't hesitate to call out to Him. He cares for you deeply
and is a prayer away.

STANDING FIRM ON YOUR KNEES

Carolyn

*He kneeled upon his knees three times
a day, and prayed, and gave thanks
before his God, as he did aforetime.*
DANIEL 6:10

One of the most beautiful memories I have of my mom was seeing her kneeling by her bed at night and offering prayers to her heavenly Father. She was a faithful prayer warrior, trusting God to care for the needs of her children, grandchildren, and many friends. She humbled herself before God, confident He heard her prayers and would answer.

During the Babylonian exile, Daniel, a Jewish man, became a favored official of King Darius. The king's other officials wanted to get Daniel in trouble, but they could find no flaw in his service or character. They devised a plan and issued a decree that everyone must pray to the king alone. But Daniel openly prayed on his knees to his God, unwavering in his commitment to honor the Lord. God protected Daniel in a den of lions! I pray I would stand firm in my faith like Daniel—even on my knees.

WORTH THE EFFORT

Suzanne

For therefore we both labor and suffer reproach,
because we trust in the living God, who is the
Savior of all men, specially of those that believe.
1 TIMOTHY 4:10

Every stage of life comes with labor and striving. If you want to excel in your career, you must be a diligent worker and put in the hours. If you want a thriving marriage, you must work at keeping communication strong and love alive. Every endeavor—whether it's raising children, running a business, or training for an athletic event—requires effort.

When a difficult task is before you, what keeps you going? Your own inner drive? A desired response from another person? Hope of a certain outcome?

Paul explains to the young pastor, Timothy, the secret to motivation in Christ's kingdom: we trust in the living God, the Savior of all. This trust in the living, risen Savior provides proper motivation for me to keep going and accomplish the things to which He's called me. On days when my efforts go unnoticed or don't seem worth it, I can carry on, knowing who I'm doing it for.

RELEASING WORRY

Suzanne

Casting all your care upon him;
for he careth for you.
1 PETER 5:7

I slipped softly into the nursery for the third time that evening. In the soft glow of the night-light, I examined the peaceful face of my sleeping baby boy. For the previous month, my husband and I had been dealing with multiple weekly doctor's appointments and changing medications to treat our firstborn son's catastrophic form of epilepsy. I often woke in the middle of the night gripped with terror over the potential outcomes.

As I tried to carry the heavy burden of my worry, terrifying scenarios filled my mind, and my trust in God's goodness was tested. As my cares grew, I felt God inviting me to lay them down. He was strong enough to carry them. He also cared for my baby more than I did.

When I laid down the burden of the worry I'd been carrying, I felt the reassurance of God's love and care. The road ahead wasn't an easy one. But God had wonderful plans for my son—and for me—that would proclaim His glory.

Sweet Fragrance of Prayer

Carolyn

*Let my prayer be set forth before thee as incense; and
the lifting up of my hands as the evening sacrifice.*
PSALM 141:2

Prayer is the most powerful resource Christians have
in maintaining an intimate relationship with God.
Discovering and discerning God's will for our lives comes
through the wisdom received from God's Word and time
spent communing with Him in prayer.

God hears and answers the prayers of His children.
Sometimes He answers yes. *I love you, and here are more
blessings than you expected.* Sometimes He answers no. *I
love you so much, but this is not My plan for you.* Other times
He answers "not yet." *I love you and I ask you to wait for My
perfect timing. Remember, I know best.*

Be encouraged, dear sister. When we are weak or
unsure of how to express our needs and desires to God,
the Holy Spirit intercedes for us in accordance with
God's will. When we pray, the words should flow from
our hearts with honesty, humility, reverence, and respect.
God delights in our prayers, and He will answer.

Love as I Have Loved

Suzanne

*This is my commandment, That ye love
one another, as I have loved you.*
JOHN 15:12

We use the word "love" so frequently, sometimes it feels like it's lost its meaning. In a single conversation, I might talk about how I love coffee, I love my husband and kids, I love my favorite TV show, and, oh yeah, I love Jesus! But my love for Jesus—and His love for me—is deep and powerful. And it's a love He asks me to extend to others.

When Jesus gave His disciples the instruction to "love one another," it was a "new commandment" (John 13:34). His friends already knew they were supposed to love their neighbors as themselves—a pretty tall order. Now their rabbi instructed, "Love as I have loved you."

That's not a love I can conjure up or fake. It's a selfless love that's passionately committed to the well-being of others—my family, my friends, my acquaintances, and even my enemies. Loving people isn't easy sometimes, but the result can be powerful, because the love comes from Him.

STRENGTH IN WEAKNESS

Suzanne

Therefore I take pleasure in infirmities, in
reproaches, in necessities, in persecutions,
in distresses for Christ's sake: for when
I am weak, then am I strong.
2 CORINTHIANS 12:10

When my children were young, I would often have discouraging days. I had nothing to complain about. My husband had a good job that provided for all our needs. My children were happy and healthy. Surrounded by so many blessings, I felt guilty and frustrated with myself for being so weak under pressure. One day I'd feel like I was doing pretty well, and the next would be disastrous.

One day my five-year-old, sensing my stress, said, "We don't worry, right, Mom? God is with us." The truth of her words struck me. *Yes, He is.* He's with us in every weak moment, failure, and doubt.

Paul took pleasure in his weakness and human struggles because he understood the secret: The more his weakness showed, the stronger he was in Christ. If today is a bad day, draw on God's strength, and remember He is with you.

THE GIFT OF FRIENDSHIP

Carolyn

A friend loveth at all times.
PROVERBS 17:17

I was an only child for eight years before my sister was born. I would create an imaginary friend named Kathy Kazoo. She enjoyed tea parties with me; was a playmate in my pretend house, school, and hospital; and was always available.

As I grew, I moved on to real—and better—friends. Over the years, these friends have deeply loved, joyfully encouraged, honestly exhorted, and steadfastly stood by me through times of joy and sorrow. Most of them also have a great sense of humor and a sweet tenderness that is shown through caring for my needs and plenty of hugs. My friends are trustworthy, giving me the confidence to share my innermost thoughts.

The Bible talks about what makes a good friend. A friend lifts you up when you fall, seeks forgiveness when needed, stands with you through trials, loves God, sharpens you in your faith, and refreshes the soul. If you have a friend like this, thank the Lord for such a precious gift.

Passing Through

Suzanne

When thou passest through the waters, I will
be with thee; and through the rivers, they shall
not overflow thee: when thou walkest through
the fire, thou shalt not be burned; neither shall
the flame kindle upon thee. For I am the LORD
thy God, the Holy One of Israel, thy Savior.
ISAIAH 43:2-3

Six years ago, we moved our young family from Colorado to California for my husband to take a new pastoral position. We left everything familiar—including our children's schools, doctors, and even family—to go where God was leading us. As we drove across Utah, the enormity of what we were doing overwhelmed me.

In Isaiah, God assures the Israelites that He will help them through any challenge they face. Big obstacles, such as navigating a serious illness, losing a loved one, or leaving a bad relationship, may seem impassable at the time. But God promises not to let any circumstance overtake you. He goes with you—His character unchanging, His resources unlimited, and His love unrestrained.

PERSISTENT PRAYER

Suzanne

*And shall not God avenge his own
elect, which cry day and night unto
him, though he bear long with them?*
LUKE 18:7

One morning my daughter came to me asking for a cup of hot cocoa. We typically don't serve the sugary drink with breakfast, so I said no. An hour later she asked again, and thirty minutes after that she once again begged for the treat. By noon, my daughter sat at the table happily sipping her cocoa with marshmallows. I had relented simply because I didn't want to deal with her request any longer.

Jesus told a parable about a persistent widow who came before an unjust judge. Day after day, the woman asked for justice against her adversary. At first the judge, who wasn't a stand-up guy, refused to help her. Finally, he became tired of her constant begging and granted her request.

The point of the story was to teach the disciples to pray and not give up. Maybe you've asked God for something 100 times. Ask 101 times! Don't give up. He cares for you and responds to persistent prayer.

SWEETER THAN HONEYCOMB

Carolyn

> *The fear of the LORD is clean, enduring for*
> *ever: the judgments of the LORD are true and*
> *righteous altogether. More to be desired are*
> *they than gold, yea, than much fine gold:*
> *sweeter also than honey and the honeycomb.*
> PSALM 19:9-10

When I first began attending church as a new believer, I was so excited to learn all I could from the Bible. I would eagerly take notes from the sermons my pastor preached so I could learn and assimilate God's beautiful truth.

The sixty-six books of the Bible are rich in law, testimony, statutes, promises, judgments, and commands. The Scriptures express the mind and heart of God, which gives life to the Christian and provides hope to the soul, joy to the spirit, and comfort to the mind. The Bible reveals all we need to know about the Trinity, our salvation, and walking with the Spirit.

Only by getting to know God's sacred Word can we live by faith. As we read it, we can obey His precepts and make strides toward trusting Him with our daily struggles. This knowledge of God's truth, and spending an eternity with Him, is worth more than gold and is sweeter than a honeycomb.

LIVING TO SERVE

Suzanne

---

*As every man hath received the gift, even so
minister the same one to another, as good
stewards of the manifold grace of God.*
1 PETER 4:10

What are your gifts? I know a woman who can cook the most amazing meals and create instant community within the walls of her home. Another friend leads Bible studies and is gifted at teaching the Bible. Still another woman ministers to others through deep, one-on-one conversations packed with biblical truth.

God has given each believer a gift she can use to serve others. These abilities may lie in the area of helping others, offering prayer support, teaching, hospitality, or something else. Maybe you've never given much thought to your gift and how to exercise it. Begin by serving in some capacity and note the things you like and dislike about the task. As you serve in different ways, you will discover the areas where you truly excel and the ministries where you are able to steward God's grace. As you faithfully exercise your gifts, your life will edify others and bring God glory.

SWEET SMELL OF THE SAVIOR

Suzanne

For we are unto God a sweet savor of Christ, in
them that are saved, and in them that perish.
2 CORINTHIANS 2:15

When we first moved to our agricultural town in the central valley of California, we noticed something odd. On certain days when you stepped outside, you were struck by the pungent, eye-watering smell of…cows, an unpleasant side effect of being downwind of several large dairies.

In contrast, on days when we received a drenching rain, the air would smell fresh and clean afterward. I came to relish the after rain smell more than I had in any other place I'd lived.

Good smells or bad, aromas connect us to our surroundings—they draw or repel us. The Christian emits an odor, the *sweet savor of Christ.* As people brush shoulders with us each day, they will "smell" something. The smell of a Christian draws some and repels others. Wherever you go, you can be sure others are catching a whiff. As you live out your faith sincerely, those being saved will be drawn to you and your life-giving fragrance.

REAL BEAUTY

Carolyn

Whose adorning let it not be that outward adorning of plaiting the hair, and of wearing of gold, or of putting on of apparel; but let it be the hidden man of the heart, in that which is not corruptible, even the ornament of a meek and quiet spirit, which is in the sight of God of great price.
1 PETER 3:3-4

Many years ago, I oversaw an overnight retreat for young girls. The theme was "Beauty from the Perspective of Scripture." I told the young women that God, who is beautiful, created and values beauty. Adornment and attitude are qualities referenced in His Word.

The Lord places less importance on outward appearance, such as our hairstyles, jewelry, and clothing. He is much more concerned about the reflection of beauty coming from a woman's heart and spirit. Does she have reverence for the Lord? Is she humble and obedient? Does she show tenderness, offer genuine love, listen intently, and look to God for her value? If the answer is yes, she possesses a rare beauty that comes from God Himself.

WRITTEN ON OUR HEARTS

Suzanne

*But this shall be the covenant that I will make
with the house of Israel; After those days, saith
the LORD, I will put my law in their inward
parts, and write it in their hearts; and will
be their God, and they shall be my people.*

JEREMIAH 31:33

Jeremiah was a prophet during a dark time for Israel.
The nation continued to ignore God's commands,
even as the people headed for His judgment in the form
of conquest by Babylon. Jeremiah had the unenviable task
of telling the rebellious people what was coming. But in
the midst of bad news, he reminds them of God's faithfulness and plans to restore them.

I love the picture of God writing His law on our hearts.
His commands make a huge difference in my life. When
the cashier treats me rudely, I can repay her with kindness. When I notice another's needs, I can give generously.
When someone frustrates me, I can choose to overlook an
offense. As I practice the commands God has written on
my heart, I feel more deeply that I am His and He is mine.

CALL TO PRAYER

— Suzanne —

*Let us therefore come boldly unto the throne
of grace, that we may obtain mercy, and
find grace to help in time of need.*
HEBREWS 4:16

German theologian and reformer Martin Luther is credited with saying, "I have so much to do that I shall spend the first three hours in prayer."

While I may struggle to maintain a consistent prayer life, prayer is important preparation for the work God has for me to do. If God's work is the engine, prayer is the fuel. Talking to God builds my intimacy with Him and allows me to actively participate in what He's doing in the world.

I often view prayer as a conversation, and it is, but Scripture reveals it is also an invitation. We are invited to come boldly to God's throne with our requests. When we do, He not only hears us, but He grants mercy and acts on our behalf! When you think about prayer as an invitation instead of an obligation, it can motivate you. With so much important work to do, it's an invitation you can't refuse.

THE CROSS OF HOPE

Carolyn

*My soul, wait thou only upon God; for
my expectation is from Him.*
PSALM 62:5

Nearly everyone who is old enough remembers where
he or she was on September 11, 2001. The terrorist
attack devastated the American people as we lost lives and
our security was shaken. When workers excavated the site
of the World Trade Center, they discovered a cross-shaped
beam that stood upright amid all the debris. It became an
improvised center of worship and a symbol of hope.

The cross is thought to be the cornerstone of the
Christian faith, providing the foundation of belief in what
Jesus did for us. The believer can go to the foot of the cross
for redemption, forgiveness, and hope for eternal life with
the Trinity. The future for a nonbeliever is complete separa-
tion from God for eternity in hell.

But Jesus's death on the cross is not the end of the story.
The manger, cross, empty tomb, and heavenly home complete the wonderful story. Even in the midst of unimag-
inable tragedy, we have a future and a hope, because our
citizenship is in heaven.

Whom Will You Serve?

Suzanne

And if it seem evil unto you to serve the Lord,
choose you this day whom ye will serve...but as
for me and my house, we will serve the Lord.
Joshua 24:15

Everyone serves something. They may serve a humanitarian cause, their employer, their passions, the pursuit of wealth, or a myriad of other things. God created us to love, serve, and glorify *Him*, but our world provides many alternative "gods" we can serve.

When Joshua led the Israelites into the land God had promised them, he reminded them of everything the Lord had done and asked them to make a choice. They could choose to serve something other than the God who had brought them out of Egypt, but they would have to decide. They would have to take a stand.

Each day we have a choice. At times our fleshly desires will tempt us to serve things other than God. We may feel as if we can serve Him *and* other things. But He requires our absolute devotion. And He is more than worthy of it.

POWERFUL PROTECTION

Suzanne

*Thy word have I hid in mine heart, that
I might not sin against thee.*
PSALM 119:11

As a child, I participated in a verse memory program, and I'm so thankful I did. Many of God's words are impressed on my heart and quickly come to mind when I face temptation or challenges. Sometimes God's Word comes to my mind in unexpected moments. I'll be going along with my ordinary day, dealing with my ordinary frustrations, and a Scripture will pop into my mind. Half the battle is knowing what God says.

When I need wisdom, I can remember that James says to ask God, who gives it generously. When I'm tempted to lie, I remember that God hates a lying tongue (Proverbs 6:17). And when I want to choose my own way instead of His, I can remember there is a wide path that leads to destruction, but God's way leads to life (Matthew 7:13). The psalmist declares that God's Word hidden in his heart acts as a deterrent to sin and a guide for righteous living. That's powerful protection in a trouble-filled world.

THE GIFT OF LAUGHTER

Carolyn

A merry heart doeth good like a medicine:
but a broken spirit drieth the bones.
PROVERBS 17:22

My husband and I were high school sweethearts, and it was his sense of humor that attracted me to him. He was famous for his jokes and storytelling, and he could always make others laugh. Since his passing, I have missed the sound of his wonderful laughter.

I see God's humor in different passages of the Bible. A donkey talks, a big fish swallows a man, and an indiscreet woman is compared to a gold ring in a pig's snout. God's humor is also evident in nature. The okapi has a giraffe head, a horse body, and zebra legs.

God knew His children needed laughter. He gave us humor to balance our lives, knowing we would experience sad and somber circumstances. As a former nurse, I know that a light heart works like medicine: It provides a decrease in blood pressure and stress, burns calories, strengthens the immune system, and releases emotionally healing endorphins. Laughter is contagious and brings both physical and spiritual refreshment.

TASTE TEST

Suzanne

O taste and see that the LORD is good:
blessed is the man that trusteth in him.
PSALM 34:8

My oldest child has always been a picky eater. For years, he has rotated through the same twenty foods, which include plain chicken, noodles, applesauce, and cereal. Over the years, it's been difficult to get him to expand his palate.

Not long ago, I decided to have him taste tortillas again. I warmed one up and put a little butter and salt on it. He protested but finally took a tiny bite. His eyes lit up. "I *love* tortillas!" he exclaimed. This experience made me wonder how many other foods he would enjoy if he would just taste them.

Sometimes God's goodness goes untasted in my life. For whatever reason, I choose not to give God a "taste test" by trusting Him as I cycle through my same favorite ways of coping. But He invites me to hand over control of my life so I can taste His goodness. Only then do I see how sweet it is to trust in Him.

TRUE FREEDOM

Suzanne

*All things are lawful unto me, but all things are
not expedient: all things are lawful for me, but
I will not be brought under the power of any.*

1 CORINTHIANS 6:12

Have you ever made a decision that was technically
okay but maybe not the best for you? Maybe you ate
a rich dessert right before bed and ended up with a stomachache. Perhaps you were low on funds and put a large
charge on a credit card, incurring debt. Or maybe you
slept in when you should have risen early to spend time in
God's Word and prayer.

The apostle Paul reminds us we are free in Christ. We
are no longer under the law but under God's grace. But
this doesn't mean that everything allowable is God's best.
In fact, Paul warns that these freedoms can become a burden when we abuse them or allow them to rule us. As a
Christian, I am under the power of the Holy Spirit of God.
As I walk in the Spirit, I receive divine wisdom to make
decisions that bring true freedom.

The Good Shepherd

——————— *Carolyn* ———————

I am the good shepherd: the good
shepherd giveth his life for the sheep.
John 10:11

In Israel, a shepherd was not highly respected. His job was considered lowly. Shepherds tended to, fed, and protected their flocks from danger and predators. The temple shepherds were more highly regarded because they cared for sheep that would be sacrificed at the temple in Jerusalem to atone for sin.

Shepherds played a prominent role in the birth of Christ. God honored them by allowing them to be the first to hear the good news. During His ministry, Jesus described Himself as the Good Shepherd, who is compassionate, caring, and unwilling to leave one sheep behind.

Not only is He the Shepherd, but Jesus is also the Lamb. John the Baptist called Him "the Lamb of God which taketh away the sin of the world." Jesus is both the Sacrificial Lamb and our Good Shepherd. He died and rose again so that we could be eternally in His loving care.

Good and Bad

Suzanne

The eyes of the LORD are in every place,
beholding the evil and the good.
PROVERBS 15:3

I powered off the TV after hearing another disheartening news story about the suffering taking place in another part of the world. I thought about my Christian brothers and sisters there and wondered what they must be experiencing and feeling. My daily concerns paled in comparison to the terror they must feel.

Just then my four-year-old ran up and hugged my legs. He smiled up at me, one eye crinkled. "I love you, Mommy!" he said. My heart leaped with joy.

Both evil and good always exist in the world. Scripture tells us that while God holds back evil on this earth (2 Thessalonians 2:7), the world is Satan's turf (Ephesians 2:2). What is important is that God sees it all—the good and the bad. There is no place on earth that is separated from His love. One day He will make all things right and destroy evil forever. In the meantime, I can trust that He sees everything and is caring for the ones He loves.

Partnering in Prayer

Suzanne

For where two or three are gathered together in
my name, there am I in the midst of them.
Matthew 18:20

A few years ago, my dad got very sick and was placed in the ICU. It was the first time either of my parents had been in a serious condition, and I was very concerned. The brief reports we received from the hospital were not encouraging.

One night, after an unsettling report, I texted my pastor's wife, Tracy, and asked if she would be praying for my dad. A few minutes later, she texted back: "Jeff and I are outside. We would love to pray with you." As we stood outside praying out loud for my dad, I felt a burden lift from my heart. Peace replaced my panic. I knew God heard us and that He would do what was best. After that night, my dad improved and was soon able to go home.

Jesus said when two or three gather in His name, He is with them. I felt Him there that night as God used dear friends to comfort me and strengthen my faith.

THE CENTER OF GOD'S WILL

Carolyn

Thy kingdom come, Thy will be done
in earth, as it is in heaven.
MATTHEW 6:10

Many years ago, my husband made a difficult decision. He changed careers to provide extra income for our family's needs. He left his teaching position at a Christian school and became a full-time businessman. He loved teaching and impacting young people for the Lord, but to be a responsible husband and father, he chose to make our needs more important than his own.

His decision greatly lessened my burden because I only had to work part-time. I considered this a true gift of love to me. He was successful in business, but I knew his heart, passion, and calling were elsewhere.

I began to pray for the opportunity for him to return to his teaching position. One day, the call came. He accepted the teaching position that would also meet our needs, acknowledging God's intervention. I'll never forget his next words: "I am delighted to be back in the business of touching lives, and I count it all joy to be in the center of God's will."

GOING TO GOD IN AFFLICTION

Suzanne

*Mine eye mourneth by reason of affliction:
LORD, I have called daily upon thee, I
have stretched out my hands unto thee.*

PSALM 88:9

The year 2020 was a hard one for me. In the midst of a pandemic, three of my four children came home from school, while the fourth was an active toddler. Kevin set up an office in our bedroom. And I lost the physical support of my friends and church family. By the end of that year, I felt like I'd been through ten years!

The psalmist understood feeling afflicted and helpless. In fact, he turned to God with these feelings every day. I was recently considering a small personal trial that causes me emotional stress. And I felt the Lord ask, "Have you asked Me to help you with that? Have you stretched out your hands to Me?" I hadn't—I felt it was too insignificant to pray about. But when I'm going through something, reaching out to my heavenly Father should be my first response. He is the One who hears me and will answer me in my affliction.

PEACEMAKER

Suzanne

*Blessed are the peacemakers: for they
shall be called the children of God.*
MATTHEW 5:9

Think of the last time you felt true peace. Maybe you
were taking a walk along a quiet forest path. Perhaps
you stood on a sandy beach watching the soothing waves
roll in. Maybe you felt at rest as you held a sleeping baby.

We search for peace in many different places: financial security, relationships, belongings, social status, and
self-care. But true peace doesn't come from any of these
sources. Real, lasting peace is found in a restored relationship with God that comes through Christ. When I start
to look to other things to provide peace, I will always be
disappointed.

When Jesus was on the earth, He preached, "Blessed
are the peacemakers." Peace is part of God's nature, and
as His children, perpetuating peace is part of our calling.
His peace stands out in a chaotic world. Those around
us—our friends, our coworkers, our neighbors—desperately need peace. How can you be a peacemaker today?

ALL THINGS NEW

Carolyn

And he that sat upon the throne said,
Behold, I make all things new.
REVELATION 21:5

There is a Japanese tradition called *kintsugi* dating back to the fifteenth century. Craftsmen use gold dust with lacquer or resin to mend broken pieces of pottery and make them whole again. The resulting creation is a masterpiece of strength and honor, often considered more beautiful than the original.

We have a heritage of salvation dating back to the first century. Our Creator and Redeemer restores sinful, broken people through the transforming blood of His Son. He delivers us from sin, makes us whole, and makes us objects of His glory.

The blood of Christ, which is more precious than gold, mends the broken relationship between God and man. It brings about the forgiveness of sins—past, present, and future—and sets us on a new path of joy, peace, and hope. The Master's merciful touch produces something new—a righteous, strong Christian who is designed to glorify the Master. If you are discouraged today, remember that God is making all things new, including your life.

LIVING WATERS

Suzanne

*For my people have committed two evils;
they have forsaken me the fountain of
living waters, and hewed them out cisterns,
broken cisterns, that can hold no water.*

JEREMIAH 2:13

How do you fix your problems? I wish I could say I go to God first, but too many times I do that only as a last resort, after I've exhausted all of my own resources. God spoke judgment on Israel through the prophet Jeremiah. The nation's problem was twofold. First, they had forsaken God, the very source of life. And second, they had turned to impotent ways of addressing their problems.

What "broken cisterns" do you harbor in your life? Do you seek connection by spending hours on social media? Do you turn to food to fill your empty places? Do you distract yourself from pain by going shopping or exercising? None of these things will ever satisfy. Only God can quench our thirst and patch up the holes in our lives. *Lord, in the brokenness of life, help me turn first and always to You, the Fountain of Living Waters.*

SIN-SIN ROLLS

Suzanne

*There hath no temptation taken you but such
as is common to man: but God is faithful, who
will not suffer you to be tempted above that ye
are able; but will with the temptation also make
a way to escape, that ye may be able to bear it.*

1 CORINTHIANS 10:13

When my son was two years old, he adorably called cinnamon rolls "sin-sin rolls." I chuckled each time he said this because of the accuracy of his word play. While a cinnamon roll is a temptation, I encounter much greater temptations than a calorie-laden pastry every single day. The temptation to gossip. The temptation to lie. The temptation to put myself ahead of others.

The good news is, I am not alone in the temptations I face. Many other people have faced and will face the same ones. Not only that, but God manages the level of my temptation and always provides a way out. His Holy Spirit can show me a better way. That's powerful truth when I'm tempted by a "sin-sin roll" or just plain sin.

ROAD TO SALVATION

Carolyn

*For whosoever shall call upon the
name of the Lord shall be saved.*
ROMANS 10:13

The choir sang "Route 66" and snapped their fingers to the rhythmic beat. My emotions were stirred, as I remembered how my husband and I had traveled some of the 2,448 miles of road also referred to as the "Main Street of America." From Chicago, Illinois, to Santa Monica, California, the Route 66 traveler can expect to create a lifetime's worth of memories.

I have traveled down another road—perhaps less familiar but of immeasurable value to me. The "Romans Road" is a group of verses penned by the apostle Paul that provides a simple gospel presentation:

- Romans 3:10, 3:23, and 6:23 explain sin and its consequences.

- Romans 5:8 and 5:12 reveal the process of redemption.

- Romans 10:9 and 10:13 define the way of salvation.

- Romans 8:38-39 provide assurance to the believer of the right road chosen.

If you, too, have traveled down this road, tell someone about it today. There is no better road.

GIFTS AND CONCERTOS

Suzanne

*Neglect not the gift that is in thee, which
was given thee by prophecy, with the laying
on of the hands of the presbytery. Meditate
upon these things; give thyself wholly to
them; that thy profiting may appear to all.*
1 TIMOTHY 4:14-15

As a child, I took piano lessons. I started out playing simple songs, but as my knowledge and technique grew, so did the complexity of the pieces of music I played. At my yearly recitals, others could see my progress.

My friend Peter began piano lessons at a young age. By high school, he practiced more than an hour a day. He expertly played beautiful concertos and won contests. Both of us made progress as pianists, but the fruit of Peter's efforts was greater because he applied himself more.

God has given each of us gifts we can use to bring Him glory. Paul encouraged Timothy to give himself wholly to his work so others might see his progress. Whatever God-given talent you possess, learn to play the "concertos." Then the world can see a powerful God at work in you.

PREPARING FOR THE LONG SIDE OF LIFE

— *Suzanne* —

*For bodily exercise profiteth little: but godliness is
profitable unto all things, having promise of the
life that now is, and of that which is to come.*
1 TIMOTHY 4:8

One of my Bible college professors used to say, "This is the short side of life." While it's easy to get caught up in the many things we hope to accomplish in our lives here on Earth, it's more important to prepare for eternity. Spiritual training, which results in godliness, is profitable for all things, including our future lives with Christ.

The secret to godliness isn't found in trying harder, just as it isn't found in sitting back and doing nothing. Godliness is cultivated as we allow God's love and acceptance to motivate us to exercise our faith. Spiritual disciplines, such as prayer, fasting, and solitude, are a gift and a blessing. They set the stage for renewal and transformation—benefiting us in the present but also in the life to come.

A WOMAN AFTER
GOD'S OWN HEART

Carolyn

*And thou shalt love the Lord thy God with
all thy heart, and with all thy soul, and
with all thy mind, and with all thy
strength: this is the first commandment.*
MARK 12:30

The heart is an amazing organ designed by God. This muscle rhythmically circulates life-giving blood to the rest of the body. When the heart is in perfect rhythm, it provides the body with optimal physical health. The heart sustains life and is the center of one's life.

A woman whose heart beats in rhythm with God's will be spiritually healthy and vibrant. Scripture shows a woman how to pursue the Lord and faithfully seek God's will in everything she does.

David was called a "man after God's own heart." Even though he made mistakes, the shepherd-king confessed wrongdoing and invited God to be present in his life. A woman after God's heart reveres, obeys, and trusts in her beloved God. When a woman loves God with her heart, soul, and mind, He uses her to bring life and health to those around her.

Tender Shepherd

Suzanne

*He shall feed his flock like a shepherd: he
shall gather the lambs with his arm, and
carry them in his bosom, and shall gently
lead those that are with young.*

Isaiah 40:11

I had been talking with a friend and mentor when she offered to pray for me. As she prayed, she thanked God for hearing our prayers, loving us, and caring. The third thought in the series stood out to me like a neon sign: *God cares.*

I'm well aware that I'm surrounded by hurting people, many of whom have suffered greater pains and losses than I. Because of this, I tend to minimize my losses, count my blessings, and try to move forward. But the heartache remains.

Maybe that's why it means so much to me that God cares. He is a tender shepherd who carries His lambs. Whatever pain you're experiencing, sit with Jesus and tell Him what you're feeling. There is no truer friend or Savior. He invites us to bring our sorrow to Him so He can hold us close and gently take us where we need to go.

Experienced Guides

Suzanne

*And the things that thou hast heard of me among
many witnesses, the same commit thou to faithful
men, who shall be able to teach others also.*
2 TIMOTHY 2:2

During a phone conversation with an older, wiser friend, I revealed some struggles I'd been dealing with. I was worried about what she might think of me, but my friend graciously explained that she had been where I am and offered some biblical advice for moving forward. "When you're in the wilderness, you need an experienced guide," she said.

All of us walk through the wilderness at times, feeling lost or disoriented. In those moments, we need help from a more experienced Christian. Maybe you *are* the more experienced Christian. Paul encouraged Timothy to replicate himself by passing on what he had learned to others and charging them to do the same.

Until the call was over, I had no idea how much I needed that conversation with someone who understood and could offer me guidance. And by investing in me, my friend prepared me to do the same for others.

Words of Healing

Carolyn

_For if ye forgive men their trespasses, your
heavenly Father will also forgive you: but if
ye forgive not men their trespasses, neither
will your Father forgive your trespasses._

MATTHEW 6:14-15

"Forgive" was the title of the sermon, and "70x7" was
emblazoned on the front cover of the bulletin—the
number Jesus gave when asked how many times a person should forgive his brother. With such a large number,
Jesus was saying to forgive into infinity, just as God has
forgiven you in Christ.

Think of our Savior on the cross of Calvary. He said,
"Father, forgive them; for they know not what they do."
Forgiveness is part of Christ's nature. Jesus taught that if
you do not forgive, your sins will not be forgiven. That is
the simple truth. Overlooking offense becomes an act of
the will, regardless of our emotions.

Sometimes we may forgive but struggle to forget.
That's when we must allow the Holy Spirit to do a work in
us. Scripture reminds us that when we accept Christ as our
Savior, our transgressions are removed as far as the east is
from the west, and our sins are cast into the depths of the
sea and not remembered. That should inspire us to forgive
others the way God forgives us.

A God Who
Delights in Mercy

— *Suzanne* —

*Who is a God like unto thee, that pardoneth
iniquity, and passeth by the transgression of the
remnant of his heritage? he retaineth not his
anger for ever, because he delighteth in mercy.*
MICAH 7:18

One day I was pulling my car into an open parking
spot at the dentist when I heard a loud *crack*. The
nose of my minivan had nicked the SUV beside me. The
owner of the vehicle, who had been on the other side of
her car, calmly walked around to the front.

Without a hint of annoyance, she listened to my
account of what had happened, and we both searched
for where the vehicles had collided. We finally discovered
a small offending scratch, just above her rear wheel well.
After a quick call to her husband, she said, "Don't worry
about it. Have a nice day!"

"Thank you," I said, my embarrassment melting into
relief.

We serve a God who delights in mercy. When we sin,
He shows us grace. Through Christ, He pardons our iniquities and overlooks our transgressions. Because of His
mercy, we don't have to languish in guilt and shame. We
can simply say, "Thank You."

CALL OF THE MIDWIVES

Suzanne

*But the midwives feared God, and did
not as the king of Egypt commanded
them, but saved the men children alive.*

EXODUS 1:17

Many years had passed since Joseph had saved all of Egypt during a famine, and his people had greatly multiplied. The Egyptians feared the Hebrews might overtake them, so the rulers issued a mandate that the midwives kill all male babies by throwing them into the Nile. Imagine receiving such grisly orders.

Since killing babies clearly went against God's law, the midwives made a bold decision: They kept doing their job. As the midwives feared God, their example encouraged others to fear Him too. Jochebed placed her baby, Moses, in a basket on the river. Moses would grow up to be the leader of God's people.

The midwives' obedience may seem like a small thing, but it was big in the purposes of God. This world needs more women like them, who don't give in to fear but revere God alone. As we fear God, we can live with purpose and inspire others to do the same.

A GIFT REJECTED

Carolyn

*For the wages of sin is death; but the gift of God
is eternal life through Jesus Christ our Lord.*
ROMANS 6:23

My children have told me that gift giving is my love language. I receive great joy from surprising my family and friends with gifts I know they like or want. I've made it a habit to look for these treasures that might make someone's day.

Several years ago, I had a longtime friend who told me I should have known she did not like me always giving her gifts. Sadly, she dismissed our friendship, which brought me great hurt and pain. I can only imagine the pain Christ feels when one whom He loves rejects His gift of salvation.

Jesus chose Judas to be one of His disciples. Judas was an eyewitness to Jesus's miraculous ministry. In a sad turn of events, Judas betrayed Christ for thirty pieces of silver. Judas rejected the gift of salvation that would come through Jesus's death and resurrection. Jesus offers you a precious gift, and He delights in your acceptance. What is your choice?

GOOD REPORT

Suzanne

The light of the eyes rejoiceth the heart: and
a good report maketh the bones fat.
PROVERBS 15:30

Not long ago I received some good news. A friend I hadn't heard from in a few years told me about an amazing answer to prayer in his life. It was one of those "God stories" that reminds you how big God is and fills you with hope. His testimony was an answer to prayers I had prayed years ago.

At times I can feel like I'm surrounded by nothing but bad news. Disappointments, grief, and heartache pile up, weighing me down. In contrast, Proverbs describes the result of good news as a light in the eyes, joy in the heart, and refreshed bones! Joyful news revives us.

I felt this when I heard my friend's good news and specific answers to prayer. It was just the reminder I needed to turn my thoughts from the bad news in my life to God's wondrous works. As Christians we already know the best news of all—that Jesus saves. Who can you share some good news with today?

PRAYING FOR PATIENCE

Suzanne

*And not only so, but we glory in tribulations
also: knowing that tribulation worketh patience;
and patience, experience; and experience, hope:
and hope maketh not ashamed; because the
love of God is shed abroad in our hearts by
the Holy Ghost which is given unto us.*
ROMANS 5:3-5

Has anyone ever warned you not to pray for patience?
"Be careful," they say. "God will bring something
hard into your life to help you develop it!"

That idea likely comes from this passage in Romans,
which clearly says that tribulation produces patience. But
what comes next is incredibly heartening! Patience leads
to experience, which leads to hope. And hope is not put to
shame as God's love is poured into our hearts by the Holy
Spirit. This whole process is beautiful and amazing—not
something to fear.

Slowing down and learning to wait on the Lord is a
blessing and allows us to practice patience, a fruit of the
Spirit. Go ahead and pray for patience—for with it comes
character, hope, and a deeper sense of God's love.

NO MYSTERY

Carolyn

*Having made known unto us the mystery
of his will, according to his good pleasure
which he hath purposed in himself.*
EPHESIANS 1:9

I love to read mystery novels and watch movies about mysteries, sleuthing to discover, through the clues presented, the solution to the underlying puzzle or the identity of the antagonist. A mystery is composed of a story with characters, setting, foundational plot, a crime or problem to solve, and finally a solution. A good mystery has red herrings—false clues—woven throughout and hints of what is to come. Of course, the climax is when the crime is solved.

The Bible is God's great story, which has the central theme of Christ and salvation. Within the pages of God's Word, the mystery of His will for mankind is revealed. From Genesis to Revelation, we can discover the unified, perfect, inexhaustible truth of His Word. Mining its wonders may require some digging, but knowing who God is and what He requires of us is no mystery. As believers, we already know the end of the story, and it's a good one.

NEW CREATION

Suzanne

*Therefore if any man be in Christ, he is a
new creature: old things are passed away;
behold, all things are become new.*
2 CORINTHIANS 5:17

My daughter loves creating things. A true artist, she can make art out of anything—a notebook, a paper plate, an old sock. She especially loves taking something ordinary and making it into something new. I'm constantly amazed by her creativity and the beautiful things she can make.

Our God is all about making things new, beginning with us. When we accept Jesus as our Savior, He makes us into new creatures. The old ways of operating—pride, envy, self-righteousness, deceit—have passed away. We no longer live for ourselves but for Christ, who was crucified for us. He miraculously transforms our very nature, changing it from decaying rot into something that is growing and bursting with life. As I watch my daughter creating with such passion, I think about how God takes pleasure in creating beautiful things too. I'm thankful that I am one of them.

STEADY SAVIOR

Suzanne

Now unto him that is able to keep you from falling, and to present you faultless before the presence of his glory with exceeding joy, to the only wise God our Savior, be glory and majesty, dominion and power, both now and ever. Amen.
JUDE 24-25

One Sunday morning, as I was walking into the darkened sanctuary, my right shin hit a solid object that caused me to lurch forward and tumble to my knees. In the darkness, I had walked right into a camera platform.

As I reflected on my epic fall, I realized that once my shin had hit that platform, there was nothing I could have done to prevent myself from falling. When it comes to walking in faith, I am also powerless to stop myself from falling into sin. The good news is, when I run into a doubt or trial or temptation, Jesus is right there to take my hand and keep me from taking a tumble. As I keep my eyes on Him, I can trust He will help me keep the faith until I reach my glorious heavenly home.

A "Nightless" Future

Carolyn

And there shall be no night there; and
they need no candle, neither light of the
sun; for the Lord God giveth them light:
and they shall reign for ever and ever.
REVELATION 22:5

While driving in my car, I listened to the words of a Bill Gaither song, "No More Night." My spirit was touched, and I began to cry. Read the words of the chorus:

No more night, no more pain.
No more tears, never crying again.
And praises to the great I Am.
We will live in the light of the risen Lamb.

These penetrating words filled me with hope. One of the hardest things I've experienced in my life was suddenly losing my husband, Randy. As a believer whose future home is with God in heaven, I find great hope in the Bible's proclamation that the night shall shine like the day. Jesus Himself will be the divine illumination. He will wipe every tear from my eye and meet every need. Because Jesus is the light of the world and no darkness can be present when He is there, my nightless future is a reason to rejoice!

A Different Kind of Friend

Suzanne

He that walketh with wise men shall be wise:
but a companion of fools shall be destroyed.
PROVERBS 13:20

When I was twelve, my dad helped me respond to an ad for raspberry pickers in the "Help Wanted" section of the newspaper. I was earning money for horse camp, and the woman my dad spoke to graciously offered me a job.

To my surprise, when I arrived on my first day, Juanita—a powerful force of a woman in her sixties—sat me in her living room with a cup of hot cocoa and charged me with guarding her house. My cushy job led to a sweet relationship with "Grandma J," as I was soon calling her. She taught me many skills, such as singing hymns, making fudge and divinity candy, and playing Rummikub. Although there was an age difference, her love for Christ was deep, and she became a lifelong friend.

Have you ever had an unlikely friendship? Maybe God is calling you to offer friendship to someone unexpected. Friends come in all ages, and a wise friend is a treasure.

What's in Your Cup?

—————— *Suzanne* ——————

And be not drunk with wine, wherein is excess;
but be filled with the Spirit; speaking to yourselves
in psalms and hymns and spiritual songs, singing
and making melody in your heart to the Lord.
EPHESIANS 5:18-19

There's a popular analogy about a cup that asks, "If I'm holding a cup of coffee and someone bumps into me, what happens?" The answer is the coffee spills out.

But why does the coffee spill out? You may be tempted to answer, "Because you got bumped!" The true answer is that coffee spilled out because coffee was in the cup. Had tea been in the cup, tea would have spilled out.

As believers, the cup of our lives is to be filled with the Spirit—so much so that we overflow with Scripture, songs, and praise! Have you ever met someone who effortlessly quotes Scripture or someone who always has a song in her heart? When those kinds of people get bumped by life, praise spills out! I want to be that kind of person—filled with the Spirit and overflowing with praise.

The Proverbs 21 Woman

Carolyn

It is better to dwell in the wilderness, than
with a contentious and an angry woman.
PROVERBS 21:19

Many of us aspire to be the woman described in Proverbs 31. In truth, she is impressive! She is a godly wife who has a noble character and who fears or reverences the Lord. She diligently cares for her home, her husband values and respects her, and her children consider her a blessing. She speaks to others with wisdom and encouragement and radiates a joyful spirit. Her home is a welcoming place of great comfort and peace.

We don't hear as much about the Proverbs 21 woman. She is mean-spirited and does not demonstrate reverence for God in her life or her relationships. She seems to work at being prideful, argumentative, and critical, causing dissension. She is a woman who complains about everything, nagging her husband "like a constant dripping" instead of showing him respect. Because she is quarrelsome, irritating, unhappy, and unrelenting in her words and behavior, her husband prefers to dwell elsewhere.

As women of faith, let's strive for a God-honoring attitude and a home rich with kindness, peace, and joy.

LET SOMEONE ELSE
DO THE BRAGGING

Suzanne

*Humble yourselves in the sight of the
Lord, and he shall lift you up.*
JAMES 4:10

I was recently interviewing a man in his eighties, and he shared some advice with me. "If you have something to brag about," he said, "let someone else do the bragging for you. It will sound a lot better coming from them!"

The Bible takes a similar approach. As beings created in God's image, we are infinitely valuable. But we must acknowledge that anything that makes us impressive comes from God and is intended to bring Him glory. Maybe that's why James tells us to humble ourselves before the Lord. Instead of seeking to elevate ourselves or further our own agendas, we should aim to please God and trust He will meet our needs for affirmation.

A pastor I know used to quote Proverbs 27:2, which says, "Let another man praise thee, and not thine own mouth." That gentleman I interviewed was right: Humility is always attractive and words of praise are best spoken by another.

SIMPLE INSTRUCTIONS

Suzanne

*But seek ye first the kingdom of God,
and his righteousness; and all these
things shall be added unto you.*
MATTHEW 6:33

I was single throughout my twenties even though I deeply desired to be married. When I attended Bible college, I assumed I'd meet my husband there. When that didn't happen, I thought I'd probably meet him at church or through my job at a Christian ministry. Instead, I made it to my thirties before meeting my husband—even as two of my younger siblings got married and one started a family.

Although my life was full of blessings, my relationship status was an area I was constantly having to submit to Christ. Regardless of my circumstances or relationship status, my purpose was simple: Seek God first. As we do that each day, He promises to add to our lives everything we need. Not some things—*all these things.* God's resources and generosity know no bounds. He had a good plan for my singleness *and* my eventual marriage. But in both states, true contentment came through seeking Him first.

A Strong Tower

Carolyn

*The name of the LORD is a strong tower: the
righteous runneth into it, and is safe.*
PROVERBS 18:10

In my living room, I have a large picture of a stately light-house located on the coast of a large waterway. The beacon light at the top of the lighthouse was designed to warn sailors of the risk of running aground and to help them guide their ships out at sea or through waterways to safety. The lighthouse served as a visible tower, its light communicating a powerful message.

In Proverbs, God's *name* is equivalent to His person. Faithful, powerful, just, merciful, gracious, all-knowing, and wise, our God is a strong tower. He is perfect in all of His ways, and His love is unfailing.

Those of us who have received the gift of salvation through faith in the birth, death, and resurrection of the Lord Jesus are deemed righteous in the eyes of God. We, as believers, can run to and trust in the security and safety of God—our strong tower in every storm.

WAITING FOR JUSTICE

Suzanne

Rest in the LORD, and wait patiently for him: fret not thyself because of him who prospereth in his way, because of the man who bringeth wicked devices to pass.

PSALM 37:7

Sometimes it can seem like the only ones getting ahead in life are those who ignore God's ways and do what's wrong. Watching the wicked prosper can be disheartening. We may even feel tempted to scrimp on character or hustle in our own strength to taste a little bit of their success.

But the Bible offers a different way: "Rest in the Lord and wait patiently for *Him*." It may feel unfair when someone who doesn't follow God's commands gets the promotion or the accolades or the perks, but we're not supposed to worry about that. God is just and fair. He sees every action, good and bad. And He does all things well in His perfect timing.

When you feel discouraged, ask God to remind you of your wealth and position as a daughter of the Most High King. Then you will be able to rest in Him and wait for His justice.

CUTTING THE
EMPTY CHATTER

Suzanne

*But shun profane and vain babblings: for
they will increase unto more ungodliness.*
2 TIMOTHY 2:16

Have you ever been in a conversation that took an unexpected turn for the worse? You're chatting about your mutual friend Mary and the challenges she's facing at home, and suddenly an edifying conversation veers into gossip? Maybe you've been part of a conversation where profanity, backstabbing, or crude language occurred. Words can be destructive and divisive.

But worse than that, the wrong kind of speech leads to ungodliness. When we find ourselves caught up in a conversation that doesn't honor God, we have two choices: We can change the conversation or leave. Both actions require courage and self-control.

Scripture reveals that our words follow what's in our hearts. If I'm struggling with the wrong kinds of conversations on a regular basis, I need to pray and ask the Lord to take my thoughts and words captive. Then I must begin the work of replacing those negative ways of communicating with words that encourage, provide joy, further God's kingdom, and lead to godliness.

An Epic Journey

Carolyn

*And Joseph also went up from Galilee, out of the
city of Nazareth, into Judaea, unto the city of
David, which is called Bethlehem; (because he was
of the house and lineage of David:) to be taxed
with Mary his espoused wife, being great with child.*

LUKE 2:4-5

The journey from Galilee to Bethlehem must have been epic for Mary and Joseph. From weather to rough terrain to danger from robbers, making such a journey was difficult and fraught with challenges, especially for a woman in late-term pregnancy. The birth of Jesus was imminent. Bethlehem is approximately seventy miles from Galilee as the crow flies, but the walking route would have been longer.

After Mary and Joseph safely arrived, they found nowhere to stay but an animal shed. It was there that the miraculous birth of Jesus took place, fulfilling the prophecy from Micah 5:2. Because Jesus was born, died, and rose again, you and I can embark on an epic journey with Him. The path may be difficult at times, but the Lord promises to go before you and be ever with you.

In Word and Deed

Suzanne

They profess that they know God; but in works they deny him, being abominable, and disobedient, and unto every good work reprobate.

Titus 1:16

When I was dating my husband, I wasn't entirely honest with him. Early in our courtship, he asked me if I liked to hike. "Sure!" I replied, even though I am a girl who usually prefers dark theaters to mountain trails. That's how I ended up on a challenging hike at dusk, where I was certain we would get lost or fall off a cliff.

A poser is someone who pretends to be something she's not to impress others. People can claim to know God, but the real evidence of faith in Christ is found in how they live. Are their attitudes and actions consistent with what they say they believe? No one is perfect, and we shouldn't pretend to be, but true, authentic faith is seen in how we live our daily lives.

Lord, let me be the kind of Christian whose actions point to my relationship with You.

READING ENCOURAGEMENT

Suzanne

*Wherefore comfort yourselves together, and
edify one another, even as also ye do.*

1 Thessalonians 5:11

After a difficult year of school during the pandemic, my second-grade daughter was struggling with reading. I kept thinking I would help her catch up by practicing with her more, but weeks slipped by with little improvement. I reluctantly reached out to a friend who lives in our neighborhood and used to work as a reading specialist at a local elementary school. She said she'd be happy to help my daughter improve her reading skills.

After the first session, my daughter came home beaming. She eagerly showed me her list of sight words to practice and read me a simple story. In sharing her knowledge and gifts, my friend had bolstered my daughter's confidence and encouraged me.

As believers, we're instructed to comfort one another. This mutual edification is a function of the body of Christ. We don't all have the same gifts, but we each have *a gift* we can use to bless God's family. How can you encourage someone today or receive comfort from another?

Devoted Heart

Carolyn

And Ruth said, Intreat me not to leave thee, or to return from following after thee: for whither thou goest, I will go; and where thou lodgest, I will lodge: thy people shall be my people, and thy God my God.
RUTH 1:16

When I became a part of my husband's family, I acquired a beautiful relationship with my mother-in-law. She expressed her love for me through quality time, special gifts, and words of encouragement in my marriage to her son.

She loved teaching and had a heart for children, including her many grandchildren. I hope she felt the extent of the love and devotion I felt for her before she passed away at fifty-three. Through her example, I learned how to be a mother-in-law to my own children's spouses.

Ruth venerated her mother-in-law, Naomi, and she showed her love and loyalty by choosing to remain with Naomi after they both lost their spouses. Ruth, who was a foreigner, was blessed with a growing faith in God, a new home in Israel, and eventually a godly husband and kinsman-redeemer, Boaz. To whom are you devoted? Think of an older woman you can bless today.

THE GIFT OF DEPENDENCE

Suzanne

*But they that wait upon the LORD shall renew
their strength; they shall mount up with
wings as eagles; they shall run, and not be
weary; and they shall walk, and not faint.*

ISAIAH 40:31

One day I was talking to my sister-in-law about some of the sad situations we knew about and I said, "I just wish I was in control."

"I don't!" she said quickly. "I don't want to be the one making all those decisions. I'm thankful God is in control."

The book of Job describes God's vast capabilities. In reality, who would want to wrestle control away from a wise and infinite God who arranged the stars in the sky, laid the foundation of the earth, and established the natural world in all of its intricacies? When we wait upon the Lord, we can have peace and hope because His wisdom and resources are vastly greater than our own. Dependence is a gift because it allows our Creator to do what is best for us. We may not always understand His plan, but when we choose to trust Him, He will give us supernatural strength to take the next step.

God's Invisible Plan

Suzanne

*But as for you, ye thought evil against me; but
God meant it unto good, to bring to pass, as
it is this day, to save much people alive.*
GENESIS 50:20

I have always loved the story of Joseph. From one angle,
Joseph's story is about a good man's hardships and trials
(until that day he became second-in-command of Egypt).
But from a big-picture view, it is a story of how God pre-
served His people, Israel, and brought them to a place
where they would become a great nation.

Trusting God, Joseph gave his best effort to every task
wherever he was no matter how unfair the circumstances.
Joseph kept the perspective that God was at work and
there was a greater story in play—one that would ultimately be for Joseph's good and God's glory.

Today, I can trust God is working through my mun-
dane circumstances in bigger ways than I know. As I trust
Him and am faithful in the small things, I can have confidence He's working out a great plan I can't see.

FISHERS OF MEN

Carolyn

And he saith unto them, Follow me, and
I will make you fishers of men.
MATTHEW 4:19

I am blessed with two handsome, smart, and talented grandsons. My older grandson is sports minded and an avid fisherman who has a bass boat, numerous fishing rods, and all the equipment and gear one needs to enjoy the sport and compete in contests. My younger grandson is an avid reader and a skilled gamer, enjoying all kinds of interactive games requiring mental acuity. Most importantly, both grandsons love the Lord and are a part of the family of God.

My heart's desire for these young men is for them to be readers of the Word and have the passion to witness and share the gospel with others, thus becoming "fishers of men." My prayer for them is to maintain a pure testimony and a strong conviction for truth. I am proud that as grandsons who are fathered by my sons, they will continue my husband's family name, but I hope they will also follow Jesus's command to bring others into the family of God by being fishers of men.

THE GREATEST LOVE STORY

Suzanne

Therefore turn thou to thy God: keep mercy and judgment and wait on thy God continually.
HOSEA 12:6

Hosea is a love story about God and His people. But it's not a pretty one. To provide a real-life illustration to His people, God told Hosea to marry a prostitute named Gomer. Gomer's unfaithfulness was a picture of Israel's infidelity to God. The nation had turned to idols and was practicing injustice.

Hosea made five proclamations of judgment on Israel, all the while personally living this cycle of sin and repentance with his adulterous wife. Despite Gomer's gross failure, Hosea still loved her, and God still loved Israel too. Though they had failed Him in many ways, He tenderly invited them to turn back to Him.

I, too, am unfaithful when I turn to other things for fulfillment or fail to live in the ways He's shown me. But His love for me never fails. When I am faithless, He remains faithful. I get to be a part of the greatest love story ever told.

Taking the
Jump with Jesus

— *Suzanne* —

I can do all things through Christ
which strengtheneth me.
PHILIPPIANS 4:13

I've never been much of a risk-taker, but as a young adult, I decided to go skydiving. When a friend who was a parachute instructor for the Air Force and had literally jumped a thousand times offered to jump tandem with me, I realized I'd never be able to go with someone I trusted more.

On jump day, we piled into a small plane, which felt like an airborne clown car, and ascended to jump altitude. Strapped together, my friend and I jumped from the plane. A thrilling forty-second free fall led into a gentle descent once our canopy opened. The views were amazing, and we landed softly several minutes later.

People have asked, "How could you jump out of a plane?" My answer is simple: I trusted the person I was jumping with. The things we can accomplish through Christ are truly amazing. When we feel safe in His hands, we can do things we never thought possible. Take a risk with Him today.

FOREVER IN LOVE

Carolyn

Husbands, love your wives, even as Christ also
loved the church, and gave himself for it.
EPHESIANS 5:25

Pictures of him adorn almost every room in my home, reminding me of my loving and godly husband. He has been rejoicing in heaven with Jesus, family, and friends for more than half a decade now.

This year, on our anniversary, I found myself reminiscing about another hot July afternoon when I married my high school sweetheart. Wedding details were cared for by my wonderful mom, since I was busy graduating and taking my nursing board exams. My dad walked me down the aisle in our hometown church as family and friends looked on. Scripture was read and music played—all preparing for the leaving and cleaving covenant of marriage.

I am thankful that Randy and I started our marriage as believers. We knew Jesus loved us, and we were bonded in that love. Randy was a sacrificial husband who sought to love me as Christ loves the church. Our love story will always be my favorite, for with the Lord, a true love story never ends. A plaque that hangs in my bedroom says it all: "You will forever be my always."

CHASING PERFECTION

Suzanne

*For in him we live, and move, and have
our being; as certain also of your own poets
have said, For we are also his offspring.*
ACTS 17:28

One day, when my daughters were young, I was trying to capture the perfect shot of them wearing their matching pajamas. I must have taken more than a dozen photos. Either the three-year-old was making a contorted face with eyes scrunched closed or the baby's hands were a total blur because she was clapping. The best photo I got had both girls looking at the camera and mostly smiling, but wisps of hair hung over the three-year-old's eyes.

I've been a perfectionist throughout my life. But over time, especially in my role as a mom, I've become painfully aware that I'm hopelessly flawed. I've asked God what He's trying to teach me through this assault on my perfectionism. And I think the answer is *dependence*. The less I can do on my own, the more I must rely on Him—the One who empowers me to do everything, even breathe. He's big enough to handle my frustrations, and He loves me deeply, imperfections and all.

A REFLECTION ON LOSS

Suzanne

*But I would not have you to be ignorant, brethren,
concerning them which are asleep, that ye
sorrow not, even as others which have no hope.*

1 THESSALONIANS 4:13

My first memories of Uncle Randy are from camping. I would wake up to hear him rustling around in the campsite, getting the coffee going and singing a little jingle.

When my uncle passed away unexpectedly six years ago, I felt the sorrow deeply. He was only two years older than my dad. My cousins, who are my age, had lost their father. Aunt Carolyn had lost her beloved husband. It was an abrupt parting.

Death is not God's original plan, and you feel that keenly when you lose someone. Though I can rejoice for my uncle, who knew Jesus, some things can never be the same here on Earth. At his memorial, the tributes and testimonies made it clear my uncle lived out the gospel. He was even the first to share the gospel with my dad, who also believed in Jesus. Though we all still feel my uncle's loss, we grieve with hope, knowing we'll see him again soon.

GOD'S POWERFUL WORD

Carolyn

*So shall my word be that goeth forth out of my
mouth: it shall not return unto me void, but
it shall accomplish that which I please, and it
shall prosper in the thing whereto I sent it.*

ISAIAH 55:11

I have a friend who is a seasoned saint with great insight,
understanding, and knowledge of God's Word. She often
wakes up in the middle of the night when she is unable
to sleep and goes to God's Word for wisdom and peace.
She has encouraged me to read the book of Proverbs, one
chapter for every day of the month. I have found Proverbs full of practical instruction on living an abundant and
prosperous life—God's way.

Every written word on the page of Scripture is spoken
to us from our heavenly Father to accomplish His purposes and perfect plan for our lives. When we realize how
much He loves us and wants the best for us, we want to
obey His instruction. His Word is powerful and always
produces results, often in a beautifully changed heart.

THE BIGGEST TREE

Suzanne

*Blessed is the man that trusteth in the LORD,
and whose hope the LORD is. For he shall
be as a tree planted by the waters, and that
spreadeth out her roots by the river, and shall
not see when heat cometh, but her leaf shall be
green; and shall not be careful in the year of
drought, neither shall cease from yielding fruit.*

JEREMIAH 17:7-8

Every summer, my family and I visit a camp located in California's Sequoia National Park. A few years ago, we drove to see the General Sherman Tree. By volume, General Sherman is the largest known single-stem tree in the world! Standing beneath the towering sequoia, which has been in place for over a thousand years, makes you feel very small.

I love how the prophet Jeremiah describes the person who trusts in the Lord. She is like a tree planted by waters, with deep roots and green leaves. This tree endures even through droughts, continuing to bear fruit. What a precious picture from God's Word. When we root ourselves in the Lord, we are truly blessed.

GOD'S GREAT LOVE

Suzanne

But God commendeth his love toward us, in that,
while we were yet sinners, Christ died for us.
ROMANS 5:8

One day a stray dog followed my husband and kids home from a walk. The little terrier mix was shaved, scratched, and caked with mud. Little white flowers clung to her eyes, making her appear possessed. She jogged on the opposite side of the road most of the walk and finally let my daughter approach her.

We decided to put her up for the night, and over the next few days, we did all we could to find her family to no avail. At first the little dog cowered each time we approached, but as my young children heaped love on "Frannie," the pup came alive, sprinting around the backyard and demanding belly rubs.

Christ died for us when we were our most unlovable. When we were stained by sin and completely helpless, His love broke in. That love transforms us, just like my children's love transformed that little dog (which a family member adopted). Praise God for His great love!

IMAGE BEARERS

Carolyn

And God said, Let us make man in our image, after our likeness.
GENESIS 1:26

I have a granddaughter who has an artistic and creative spirit. She enjoys drawing, painting, ceramics, and other art forms. She is grateful for the compliments from her art teachers, but she knows that God is responsible for her giftedness in art and endeavors to do her best for Him.

God is the Great Artist, from whom all creativity in the world flows. Heaven, earth, sun, moon, stars, oceans, fish, birds, animals, and of course mankind were created by our perfect God. When God saw all He had created, He was pleased and said it was good.

God created humans as His image bearers. What a privilege to reflect God and His character to others and to glorify Him through our words and deeds and creativity. These things point others to their Creator and Savior. He created each of us with unique talents and areas of giftedness we can use to honor Him.

KILLING MY DREAMS

Suzanne

*But as it is written, Eye hath not seen, nor
ear heard, neither have entered into the
heart of man, the things which God hath
prepared for them that love him.*

1 CORINTHIANS 2:9

As a single woman in my thirties, I had not yet realized my greatest desires. Though I had a fulfilling job and good friends, I would not be a young bride or mother like I'd imagined.

I had a choice to make: I could dwell on the deep sense of loss I felt at the death of those dreams, question God's goodness, and become bitter. Or I could grieve the things I would not be and ask my loving Father to show me new dreams—the things "eye hath not seen." By God's grace, I chose the latter.

As a single woman, I could still be fruitful. I could have divinely orchestrated conversations. I could serve those in need. I could bring sweetness to bitter situations. As I let go of my expectations for my life and allowed God to take control, He showed me the amazing things He had been doing all along.

PARTY IN HEAVEN

Suzanne

*I say unto you, that likewise joy shall be
in heaven over one sinner that repenteth,
more than over ninety and nine just
persons, which need no repentance.*
LUKE 15:7

The best party I ever attended was my wedding reception. It was held in a beautiful, remodeled barn with giant picture windows. We ate tri-tip for dinner and monogrammed cupcakes for dessert. But the best part of the event was seeing the friends and relatives who joined us to celebrate our marriage. It was a joyous occasion I will never forget.

The Bible talks about a party in heaven. Angels gather and rejoice every time a sinner repents. Think about the moment you repented of your sin and followed Christ. When you gave your life to Him, there was a giant celebration in heaven!

I want to celebrate what God celebrates. As His follower, I can participate in these joyous conversations by telling others the good news and sharing the hope that I have in Him. And when someone follows Christ, I can join the celebration.

Sweet Comfort

Carolyn

*Who comforteth us in all our tribulation, that
we may be able to comfort them which are
in any trouble, by the comfort wherewith
we ourselves are comforted of God.*
2 CORINTHIANS 1:4

After my husband died, I received calls from other widows who desired to minister to me by bringing a meal or just having a conversation. Through their empathy, those women were a true blessing. They had walked the road I walked and could provide some expert understanding and personal advice.

They were able to listen and allowed me to be myself and grieve for my beloved without feeling awkward. These friends offered me God's comfort, and I will forever be grateful for this act of love.

Now it is my turn. Because I have lost a spouse, I can come alongside others who are widowed and offer the comfort God provided me through my friends. I can minister to them by listening, consoling, wiping away the tears, and being available.

CAUGHT CHOCOLATE-HANDED

—— *Suzanne* ——

But if ye will not do so, behold, ye
have sinned against the LORD: and be
sure your sin will find you out.
NUMBERS 32:23

When I was a kid, we rarely had sweets around the house. One treat my mom did buy was giant chocolate muffins. She would buy a dozen, wrap them individually in plastic, and freeze them. Each Saturday, she'd defrost a few to go with our breakfast.

One day I was craving sugar, so I sneaked into the garage and snagged a muffin. Conviction set in the moment I took the contraband to my downstairs bedroom. As I was headed back to the scene of the crime with the stolen goods, my mom spotted me. "What do you have there?" she asked with a raised eyebrow. I quickly confessed the whole story.

That wasn't the last time I've been caught in my sin. God says that sin against Him, which is all sin, will always be found out. It may not happen right away, but it will be discovered eventually. That's a good reason to stop hiding, confess sin, and seek God's forgiveness.

WHEN FAILURE COMES

Suzanne

*And such trust have we through Christ
to God-ward: not that we are sufficient
of ourselves to think any thing as of
ourselves; but our sufficiency is of God.*
2 CORINTHIANS 3:4-5

Have you ever felt like you're failing at life? Maybe you have a lot of balls in the air, and you keep dropping them. I have more stories than I can count of when I forgot something important, overcommitted and under-delivered, and let others down, including my own family.

Feelings of missing the mark come naturally to humans. That's because apart from God, each of us is deeply inadequate. We are insufficient to save ourselves and even to do any good works (Isaiah 64:6) apart from Christ.

In fact, we were never intended to carry the burden of cultivating a perfect life or image. Our imperfection points us to the perfect One. As we focus on the sufficiency of our Savior and His sacrifice, we can live freely, depending on Him to get the wins and praising our all-sufficient Lord.

IT'S NOT ABOUT ME

Carolyn

That at the name of Jesus every knee should bow, of things in heaven, and things in earth, and things under the earth; and that every tongue should confess that Jesus Christ is Lord, to the glory of God the Father.
PHILIPPIANS 2:10-11

My favorite hymn is "How Great Thou Art." It beautifully gives honor and glory to God with these words:

Then I shall bow in humble adoration,
And there proclaim, My God, how great Thou art!

My soul rejoices that God loved me so much that He gave His Son to die on the cross to take away my sins. Now I am His, and I am worthy to address Him as my Father. My purpose in life is to glorify Him. While it's easy to get caught up in my own busy life, cares, and concerns, this life is not about me—it is about my glorious God and Savior.

With joy in my heart, I can lean on God daily, worshiping and thanking Him in all circumstances.

Origin Story

Suzanne

So God created man in his own image,
in the image of God created he him;
male and female created he them.
GENESIS 1:27

Recently I watched a movie that came out fifteen years ago. Wondering what had happened to the vivacious young starlet who starred in the film, I did a little research. Like too many successful actresses, she was in rehab (again). In one interview, she talked about hitting a low point immediately after the success of one of her movies.

I sometimes believe that if I achieve certain standards of success, I'll feel worthy. But that's simply not true. Feelings of worthlessness can strike those who appear to be wildly successful just as easily as they do the average person.

But our value is intrinsic; we are created in the image of God! When we look to Him for our worth, we will never be disappointed. He loved us so much He died for us. The next time you feel worthless, remember your origin story. You are more valuable to God than you could imagine.

What I Want to Do

Suzanne

*For we know that the law is spiritual: but I
am carnal, sold under sin. For that which
I do I allow not: for what I would, that
do I not; but what I hate, that do I.*
ROMANS 7:14-15

One day, my four-year-old son offered a shockingly honest response after I corrected him.

"But I want to do it," he replied.

"I know you do," I said, stifling a laugh, "but the answer is no!"

My young son articulated exactly what the apostle Paul talked about in Romans 7. Even as a Christian, I am carnal, and at times, "what I hate, that do I." This battle against sin is a lifelong struggle. The good news is that I have help to say no to sin. When I just "want to do it," the Holy Spirit can help me do what is right.

Unlike me, God doesn't laugh when His children are tempted to give in to their selfish, sinful desires, because He knows the havoc sin wreaks on our lives. But He does offer forgiveness and the grace for us to make better choices the next time temptation comes.

THE GREATEST KINDNESS

Carolyn

*But after that the kindness and love of God
our Savior toward man appeared.*
TITUS 3:4

In *A Volume of Friendship*, copyright 1912, I found these words from an anonymous writer: "Kind hearts are the gardens. Kind thoughts are the roots. Kind words are the blossoms. Kind deeds are the fruits."

This writer expresses so beautifully how the heart and mind work together to produce kind words and actions. Showing kindness to others should be a daily exercise for all of us to endeavor.

As we walk with the Spirit, we will produce the fruit of kindness, which is tenderness, gentleness, and a gracious, benevolent spirit toward others. Our heavenly Father set the ultimate example when He provided a way of salvation through Jesus Christ. His was the greatest act of kindness the world has known. As a believer, I hope to reflect that kindness that will draw others to God.

Working for More

Suzanne

*And whatsoever ye do, do it heartily, as
to the Lord, and not unto men.*
Colossians 3:23

My first job out of college was working for a large
Christian organization as a children's magazine
editor. When you're writing words to encourage believers (or serving in the church, like my husband, who is
a pastor, does), it's easy to see how your work is contributing to the kingdom. But most believers don't work in
a strictly Christian environment. I have friends who are
nurses, teachers, mechanics, artists, carrot farmers, engi-
neers, stay-at-home moms, and administrative assistants.

Whatever your "job" is—even if you're retired—you
can do it as unto the Lord. The beauty of working for
Christ is you don't have to stress over work politics, climb-
ing the corporate ladder, or even work output. Your task is
simple: Work hard for the Lord and not people.

At times we may feel like the purpose of work is simply
to pay the bills, but we're created to find purpose and satis-
faction through our labor, ultimately, to bring God glory.

MITIGATING MY HEART

Suzanne

*Watch and pray, that ye enter not into temptation:
the spirit indeed is willing, but the flesh is weak.*
MATTHEW 26:41

When I lived in Colorado, two large forest fires devastated our community. In both fires, my friends lost their homes. A former coworker had less than an hour to gather what keepsakes she could before being evacuated. Afterward, she spent months living in a hotel and dealing with insurance before a new home was built.

Through those tragedies, I learned about wildfire mitigation, the process of taking precautions to protect a building from fire. For example, one might clear any dry trees or brush near the home, making it easier to defend it during a fire.

What does it look like to mitigate against sin, a force more destructive than wildfire in our lives? First, we must be alert to temptation and situations where we are likely to sin. Second, we must be in prayer about our weaknesses, asking the Father to "deliver us from the evil one" when the fire comes. As we mitigate our hearts, we exercise wisdom and give the enemy a smaller target.

Numbering My Days

———— *Carolyn* ————

Thine eyes did see my substance, yet being
unperfect; and in thy book all my members
were written, which in continuance were
fashioned, when as yet there was none of them.
PSALM 139:16

Our church went through a very traumatic time when our young pastor died after being diagnosed with COVID-19. His ministry had been growing within the church and online, impacting many for the Lord all over the world. His beautiful wife and young daughter know his death was in God's perfect plan, but their grief is great.

God's Word tells us that He established the number of our days of life on this earth before we were even born. In His sovereignty, God not only created us in our mother's womb, but He also ordained the time we would live and the specific time we would die. No human intervention can change God's timetable. As one young widower said, "We don't know if we're old or young. Only God does." If we accept that we have no control but our infinitely loving and good heavenly Father does, we can live an abundant life, making each day count for God.

GOD-SIZED DREAMS

Suzanne

Delight thyself also in the LORD: and he
shall give thee the desires of thine heart.
PSALM 37:4

People love to talk about following their dreams. That may sound good, but God doesn't call us to follow our dreams. Our dreams aren't that important. What is important is God's glory, which is achieved as we walk in His ways.

That doesn't mean He doesn't care about our dreams. He gives His children good gifts. I and so many others have realized the dreams of our hearts. As a teenager, I wanted to work for a Christian magazine. God allowed that dream to come true, even providing for me to work for the publisher I had in mind! I desired a husband and family, and though the fulfillment of that dream was delayed, God eventually supplied those things in His perfect timing.

Other dreams have fallen by the wayside, but that's okay. As I delight myself in the One who created me and loves me, He gives me new, God-sized desires. True joy is not found in following my dreams; it's found in following Him.

WISDOM AND FOOLISHNESS

Carolyn

The fear of the LORD is the beginning of knowledge:
but fools despise wisdom and instruction.
PROVERBS 1:7

The magazine ad was catchy. It described an easy fix for
weight loss, a topic with which I was *obsessed* during
my early twenties. Just buy this outfit that resembled an
astronaut suit and attach your vacuum cleaner to the con-
nector point, the ad claimed. Turn your vacuum on, and
the fat in your body would be sucked right out. I can't
believe I thought this would work, but I did.

Fortunately, the two people with whom I spoke about
it had wisdom and common sense and talked me out of
purchasing this foolish, unscientific "quick fix."

Respect for God is the start of wisdom. Believers who
seek God's wisdom will receive it, and the truths gained
in Scripture will provide the foundation for learning
and knowledge. Proverbs offers the principles of discipline, self-control, and prudence. These principles may
be applied to every area of life. A person who seeks true
wisdom will find success in life and please God.

A Date with Dentistry

Suzanne

What time I am afraid, I will trust in thee. In
God I will praise his word, in God I have put my
trust; I will not fear what flesh can do unto me.
PSALM 56:3-4

have a complicated relationship with the dentist. Most
people don't *relish* going to the dentist, but I have an out-
right fear. Several years ago, I had to get a cavity filled. As I
attempted to hold my mouth open wide, while numb, for
thirty minutes, memories of past dental stress came flood-
ing back. And sitting in that dentist chair, hands clammy,
drill buzzing, I found myself on the brink of coming
unglued. I got through it, but I left hoping I wouldn't
have to return anytime soon.

All of us become afraid at times (about bigger things
than getting a cavity filled). But God is far more powerful
than anything I fear. Nothing can hurt me unless it is His
will. As I recognize His sovereignty over my life and trust
in Him, I truly have nothing to fear.

THE GLORY OF GRANDMOTHERS

Carolyn

*With the ancient is wisdom; and in
length of days understanding.*
JOB 12:12

When I was seven, both of my grandmothers joined my mom, dad, and me on a road trip to Sarasota, Florida. I was totally pampered sitting between both of my loving grandmothers in the back seat of our car. After reaching our destination, we put on our bathing suits and headed to the beach.

My paternal grandmother fearlessly swam too far out in the ocean, and my father had to rescue her. My maternal grandmother was afraid someone would steal her money, so she pinned her paper money into her bathing suit and ended up ironing her wet money later. Clearly, I have fond memories of this childhood vacation.

A familiar grandmother in the Bible is Lois, the mother of Eunice and grandmother of Timothy. Her deep and enduring faith in the Lord and her priority in training Timothy in the Scriptures was her legacy. Amid a culture of immorality and pagan beliefs, Lois stood out as an example of righteous living. Her wisdom greatly benefited Timothy and the founding of the early church.

BE OF ONE MIND

Suzanne

Now I beseech you, brethren, by the name of
our Lord Jesus Christ, that ye all speak the same
thing, and that there be no divisions among
you; but that ye be perfectly joined together in
the same mind and in the same judgment.

1 CORINTHIANS 1:10

My daughters, who are two years apart, have a penchant for arguing. Some days it feels like they're arguing about *everything*. As their parent, it's disheartening to see them not getting along. My best days as a mom are the ones where they're kind and generous toward each other.

I've recently noticed a lot of divisions cropping up among believers. We have different views on cultural issues. We disagree on how to interpret doctrine. We even bicker over what music should be played in church. We all love Jesus and believe the gospel, but we divide over many secondary things.

Paul pleaded with the Corinthians to be of one mind. Their unity proclaimed a risen Savior who could truly break down barriers between people. As we seek unity with fellow believers, we honor our Father.

LOOK WHO'S TALKING

Carolyn

*For it is not ye that speak, but the Spirit
of your Father which speaketh in you.*
MATTHEW 10:20

When my husband passed away, my pastor graciously accepted my request for him to give the message at the memorial service. In front of many unsaved family members and friends, his was one of the clearest and most beautiful gospel messages I had ever heard. When I thanked him for his ministry and message that day, my pastor said he could not even remember what he had said.

The Lord had given him the perfect words to share with our family and friends. I was so blessed by my faithful pastor who had humbly acknowledged and honored the Lord with his words.

God's Word reassures believers that as we humbly submit to the guidance of the Holy Ghost and allow God to use us to do His will, the Holy Spirit will instruct us on what to say in the moment (Luke 12:12). I can witness boldly and talk about God's Word with others because it's not me talking but God the Spirit.

THE GREATEST HAPPINESS POSSIBLE

Suzanne

*And I will delight myself in thy commandments,
which I have loved. My hands also will I lift
up unto thy commandments, which I have
loved; and I will meditate in thy statutes.*
PSALM 119:47-48

Psalm 119 is a prayer of the one who delights in and lives by God's Word. "Delight" isn't always a word we associate with the Bible. We may tend to view God's law as something rigid and difficult to obey. But it is so much more than that.

I remember being moved by a video about Iraqi believers receiving the Bible in their own language for the first time. One woman equated receiving the Bibles to an Iraqi saying that went something like this: "I thought that when I saw my beloved, I would experience the greatest happiness possible. But now that he is here with me, that happiness is exceeded."

That woman's passion challenged me. Do I have the same passion for God's Word? Do I love and appreciate it the way she did? Like this woman and the psalmist, I want to be a lover of God's beautiful Word.

Just Do It

Carolyn

...be strong, and do it.
1 Chronicles 28:10

My daughter-in-law Jill recently shared with me how this verse had impacted her life during a very challenging time. She, my son, and their family had moved back to Ohio from Indiana. The stresses of packing and selling their home, moving away from friends, looking for a new house, preparing to homeschool their two children, starting my son's new business, reestablishing in a different neighborhood, and finding a new church family were overwhelming. Each day with God's strength, Jill successfully moved forward with purpose to fulfill His exhortation to "do it."

Scripture is full of ordinary characters who accepted the charge of accomplishing God's will. Noah built the ark. Joshua led the Israelites to the promised land. Esther fearlessly approached the king and saved the Jewish people from annihilation. David fought and killed Goliath. Jesus, our extraordinary Savior, did His Father's will through His death and resurrection. When life feels overwhelming, we can follow our Savior's example and simply do what needs to be done.

Redeem the Time

Suzanne

*See then that ye walk circumspectly, not
as fools, but as wise, redeeming the
time, because the days are evil.*
EPHESIANS 5:15-16

How do you spend your time? Many of us spend time
working, sleeping, exercising, watching TV, relating
to friends, and engaging in an assortment of other activities. Many of these things we use our time on are good
things. But are they the best things?

I once heard a speaker say, "Schedule first what matters most." Think about some of your top priorities.
Maybe you want to spend time reading the Bible every
day. Perhaps you want to connect more deeply with family members. Or maybe you feel like church is important
to you. Whatever your top priorities are, put them on
your calendar first. Commit to the time you will attend
church. Schedule quality time with your children or the
people you care about. Make Bible reading the first task
of your day.

Each of us is given a limited number of days to live on
this earth and do God's will. Choose wisely and redeem
the time.

WHITER THAN SNOW

Carolyn

Purge me with hyssop, and I shall be clean:
wash me, and I shall be whiter than snow.
PSALM 51:7

I had an opportunity to go swimsuit shopping with my sweet, oldest granddaughter. She and I enjoy time together, often making each other laugh. We found a beautiful suit that was white with blue stripes. She tried it on, and it fit her perfectly, so we purchased the suit.

Unfortunately, after several times in the pool, the chlorine washed away the blue stripes from the suit. My granddaughter still wears the swimsuit, but it is pure white, like snow.

This swimsuit situation caused me to think about the spiritual cleansing of our sins that Jesus's stripes made possible. Through the prophet Isaiah, the Lord said, "Though your sins be as scarlet, they shall be as white as snow" (Isaiah 1:18). Because Jesus was flogged and bloodied for us, we can be cleansed from all unrighteousness through simple faith. We now are clothed in His righteousness, spotless and blameless, whiter than snow. Praise Him!

A Fruitful Life

Suzanne

*I am the vine, ye are the branches: He that abideth
in me, and I in him, the same bringeth forth
much fruit: for without me ye can do nothing.*
JOHN 15:5

My pastor recently preached a message about the importance of reading Scripture for the purpose of spiritual growth. "When I need to lose twenty pounds, I'm always looking for instant results," he said. "But it's not instant. I have to make choices day after day that support my goal."

Getting results in our spiritual lives works the same way. If you want a close, vibrant relationship with God, you must choose daily to spend time in His Word. You must talk to Him in prayer and listen in stillness to hear His answer. A thriving relationship with Jesus doesn't happen overnight. It is carefully cultivated day after day until the branches begin to produce fruit.

California, where I live, produces a lot of fruit. The fruit is only as good as the vine or the tree to which it's attached. To bear good fruit, we must abide in a good Savior, a Savior who gave everything for us.

OVERCOMER

Carolyn

Ye are of God, little children, and have
overcome them: because greater is he that
is in you, than he that is in the world.

1 JOHN 4:4

One of my favorite exercises is walking. I use a wrist tracker to count my steps, as I try to reach 10,000 steps a day. Sometimes, my mind and body are in sync, and I reach my goal. Other times, I struggle to overcome my lack of perseverance. When I successfully follow the plan, I gain a victory that results in a happier, healthier me.

In 1 John, the apostle encourages believers that they are of God and can overcome false teachers. He had spent much of the book warning the followers of Jesus to beware of false, unbiblical teaching. Such teachers have the spirit of the antichrist, which is Satan.

What does it look like to be an overcomer? Even in the midst of hard circumstances and false teaching, we have the spirit of the living God, who lives in us and helps us discern truth from lies, light from dark, and good from evil. Satan knows defeat because we are overcomers!

BIG GIRLS DO CRY

Suzanne

They that sow in tears shall reap in joy.
PSALM 126:5

One day, during a work meeting, I cried unexpectedly. We had discussed something near to my heart. Things got heated, and a combination of lack of sleep and my emotion for the subject conspired to obliterate my professional demeanor. I was so embarrassed.

Why, Lord? I thought in frustration. *Why didn't You give me the strength to keep it together?* Instead, I was sure my blubbering had damaged my credibility. Culture tells us that those who keep an iron command of their emotions exhibit strength, while those who cry are seen as soft. Why else would speakers and pastors apologize when they choke up? They're showing weakness.

Many heroes of the faith were weepy: Jeremiah the "weeping prophet," King David, Paul, and even Jesus cried. Tears aren't just some inconvenient bodily function. Tears can demonstrate repentance and a tender heart. Tears cleanse and heal. Tears impact others and are noticed by the Lord. Tears are part of being human. Sometimes big girls do cry, and that's okay.

The Road to Refreshment

Carolyn

The liberal soul shall be made fat: and he that watereth shall be watered also himself.
PROVERBS 11:25

W ho or what is your daily source of refreshment? Do you turn to entertainment or perhaps to a stress-relieving routine?

One day, during my morning devotions, I came across Proverbs 11:25, which talks about refreshing others to be refreshed. I took the opportunity to write an uplifting note to a friend. Later that day, my spirit was encouraged and refreshed by my granddaughter, who read aloud Psalm 100 during our time together. God used His Word, spoken by my granddaughter, to energize, strengthen, and refresh me mentally and physically.

In the book of Proverbs, the Lord uses simple analogies to illuminate His truth. One of them is this idea that the generous person who refreshes others will thrive and prosper. Think about the importance of water to growing things. Farmers depend on rain to water their crops. A garden needs water for vegetables to grow. Water nourishes, invigorates, and refreshes the plant. Following God's Word and refreshing others will result in abundant blessings and eternal refreshment.

BE A LIGHT

Suzanne

Do all things without murmurings and
disputings: that ye may be blameless and
harmless, the sons of God, without rebuke, in
the midst of a crooked and perverse nation,
among whom ye shine as lights in the world.
PHILIPPIANS 2:14-15

When I think about murmuring and disputing, I think of the Israelites. While they were under oppression as slaves in Egypt, they complained that God had forgotten them. Then, when God answered their cries and miraculously freed them from slavery in Egypt, the people continued to gripe every chance they got.

Compared to Israel, my complaints seem small: Perceived mistreatment by another person. Less-than-ideal circumstances in my personal life. Not getting things I believe I deserve. But I can easily become dissatisfied with such things and start to complain and argue.

Paul says that doing things *without* murmuring and disputing sets believers apart—so that they *shine* like brilliant lights. How incredible! The world is full of complainers, but you can choose to be a light instead.

Redeemed

Carolyn

*For ye are bought with a price: therefore glorify God
in your body, and in your spirit, which are God's.*
1 CORINTHIANS 6:20

Have you ever walked through a cemetery and read the inscriptions on the gravestones? I saw one on a monument that was simple, but for me, it said it all: "Redeemed." Even in death, this precious soul offered a testimony to the Lord.

One definition of "redeem" is to "save someone from sin, error, or evil." This is certainly a proper understanding of the word from the Christian perspective. In the hymn "I Will Sing of My Redeemer," Philip P. Bliss writes about Christ's wondrous love in suffering on the cross to set us free from the curse. The song expresses the beautiful truths that Christ's blood purchased, pardoned, and paid the debt for our sin, resulting in our freedom and redemption.

In His power, love, and mercy, Jesus was victorious over sin and death, restoring our relationship with the Father. Because Christ's blood has bought us for God, we honor Him with our bodies and our souls.

A REAL BEAUTY

Suzanne

Thou art all fair, my love; there is no spot in thee.
SONG OF SOLOMON 4:7

"You're a real beauty." My four-year-old son's earnest words warmed my heart.

Most days I don't feel beautiful, at least not compared to the women I see on TV or even rub shoulders with. I regularly doubt my beauty. It's much easier to focus on my flaws than to acknowledge that God makes beautiful things and therefore has made me beautiful.

In Song of Solomon, King Solomon uses poetic language to express his adoration for his beloved. The book features elaborate descriptions of her beauty, and we see her self-confidence blossom under the attention of her beloved. "My beloved is mine, and I am his," she concludes (2:16).

Song of Solomon is also a picture of how God loves us, His daughters. He finds us beautiful. Not in a cheesy, love song kind of way. We are beautiful to Him because He created us, and He sees our inner character *and* outward beauty. Never forget that He looks at you and says, "You're a real beauty."

Walking in the Footsteps of Jesus

— *Carolyn* —

He that saith he abideth in him ought
himself also so to walk, even as he walked.
1 JOHN 2:6

During my trip to Israel, I walked the route in the Old City of Jerusalem called the Via Dolorosa. Translated as "Way of Suffering," it is the path believed to be taken by the Savior as He carried His own cross to Golgotha. For me, this was a humbling and sobering journey on foot, retracing Jesus's steps from over 2,000 years ago.

In ancient times, a disciple was to follow in his rabbi's footsteps so closely that the dust from the master's steps got on his sandals. Jesus is our perfect example and the One we imitate in our words and actions. Surrendering to God's will is the first step toward walking with Christ.

Christ kept the commandments and demonstrated unconditional and sacrificial love. He spoke truth. He was patient, humble, and compassionate. Most of all, He valued people. These are the characteristics of Christ we must emulate. As believers, we have big shoes to fill. Let's follow so closely that our feet get dirty.

FINISHING STRONG

Suzanne

---

*I have fought a good fight, I have finished my
course, I have kept the faith: henceforth there
is laid up for me a crown of righteousness,
which the Lord, the righteous judge, shall
give me at that day: and not to me only, but
unto all them also that love his appearing.*

2 TIMOTHY 4:7-8

I used to think it was a good idea to run even when no one
was chasing me. This led me to sign up for, and complete,
three half-marathons. No matter how hard I trained or
how in shape I was, that last mile or two was always difficult. At the end of one race, a friend kept me going by
singing a boisterous version of "My Favorite Things" from
The Sound of Music.

Sometimes I feel fatigue creeping into my spiritual life.
As I run the race, I become discouraged and lose energy. I
may even wonder if it's worth it to keep running. Oh, but
it is! The apostle Paul says he looks forward to the crown
of righteousness the Lord will give him on that day. God
and a cloud of witnesses are cheering us on. As I dwell in
His Word, I can finish the race and keep the faith.

ONE-
MINUTE
PRAYERS
for Women

Draw Near to God Today

Reach out to God with praise and thanksgiving using these thoughtful and insightful prayers.

This delightful collection of one-minute talks with God will help you share your heart's desire to walk with Jesus, grow spiritually strong, reach out to others, and find comfort.

Whether you start your morning with God, find strength in the middle of the afternoon, or close your day with Him, you'll experience His peace, embrace His grace, and find joy in His presence.

*Cause my faith to grow, Lord. Each day that I
come to meet with You, may I know You better.
Replace my ignorance with Your knowledge.
Help me be strong in my commitment to You.*

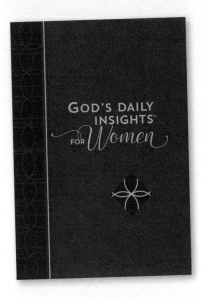

This daily devotional sheds light on the truths about God revealed in Scripture, providing a better understanding of who God is and what He is doing in your life.

As you encounter God and the Bible, do you find yourself having more questions than answers? This devotional was written with you in mind. Each day you'll learn something new about God and how that truth applies to you.

Whatever you need—a new beginning, patience while you wait, strength to make a difference, or wisdom for a difficult decision—God has an answer waiting for you to find. Start your journey of discovery today.

"My prayer is that this will be one of the most exciting years of your life."

LLOYD JOHN OGILVIE

Don't Settle for Anything Less

A lot has changed since this timeless devotional was first released almost 40 years ago, but one truth has stayed the same—a loving Savior still calls you closer to Him and wants His very best for you. Will you accept His gracious invitation?

These short yet powerful devotions will take you less than 10 minutes each to read, but their impact on your daily life will be incalculable. As you fellowship with God and learn more about Him, you'll experience anew His grace, mercy, wisdom, and more.

This beautifully designed edition of this classic devotional makes an ideal gift or a great way to rededicate yourself to spending more time in God's presence.

Are you ready to experience His best? Start today.

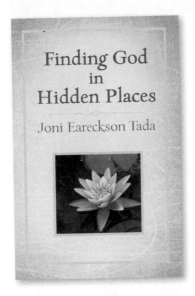

Finding God in Hidden Places

Joni Eareckson Tada

Join bestselling author and artist Joni Eareckson Tada on a deeply personal journey as she explores the presence of a holy God in hidden places.

Stories from Joni's life shine in this collection of gathered memories. You will recall quiet, out-of-the-way moments in their own life when God was present—both in happy and sad times. Words of encouragement, comfort, and insight will leave your soul satisfied and longing to be closer to your loving Father, who often shows up when least expected.

Finding God in Hidden Places is the perfect size for bedtime reading or taking along for daytime moments of rest and reflection.

To learn more about Harvest House books and
to read sample chapters, visit our website:

www.HarvestHousePublishers.com

HARVEST HOUSE PUBLISHERS
EUGENE, OREGON